Nova Scotia Beaches, Parks & Natural Sites

Patty Mintz

Co-published by
The Province of Nova Scotia
and Nimbus Publishing Limited

Co-published by the Province of Nova Scotia and Nimbus Publishing Limited.
Sponsored by:

Economic Development and Tourism
A product of the Nova Scotia Government Co-publishing Program

Design: Arthur Carter, Halifax
Photo Credits: Photos are courtesy of Nova Scotia Economic Development and Tourism. The images on page 14 are courtesy of the Kentivlle Development Corporation; those on pages 74–75 are courtesy of Dave Stephens; those images on pages 78, 82–83 are courtesy of the Region of Queens Municipality.
Cover Photo: Kejimkujik National Park, courtesy of Nova Scotia Economic Development and Tourism.

Printed and bound by Printcrafters Inc.

Canadian Cataloguing in Publication Data
Mintz, Patty
Discover Nova Scotia, beaches, parks and natural sites
Co-published by N. S. Dept. of Economic Development and Tourism.
Includes bibliographical references and index.
ISBN 1-55109-258-4
I. Parks—Nova Scotia—Guidebooks. 2. Natural areas—Nova Scotia—Guidebooks. 3. Nova Scotia—Guidebooks. I Nova Scotia. Dept. of Economic Development and Tourism. II. Title.

FC2307.M56 1998 917.1604'4 C97-950254-3
F1037.M56 1998

Dedication
To Bill, Caileigh, Minga, and Wolf, who make returning home a happy occasion. To my parents for their undying support.

Nimbus Publishing acknowledges the financial assistance of the Canada Council and the Department of Canadian Heritage.

Contents

Evangeline Trail

Glooscap Trail

Sunrise Trail

Ceilidh Trail

Cabot Trail

Fleur-de-lis Trail

Marconi Trail

Marine Drive

Halifax Dartmouth

Lighthouse Trail

Acknowledgements

A sincere and hearty thank you to the many people who contributed information and offered advice, who proofread copy, sent material, or agreed to an interview. In particular, I wish to thank Brian Kinsman, Chris Trider, Rosemary Eaton, Elizabeth Corser, Marian Zinck, Betty O'Toole, Bob Grantham, Ron Williams, Pat Murphy, Bob Bancroft, Doug Archibald, Martha Devaney, Herb Berry, Sharon Ingalls, Shirley Smith, Danielle Wharton, Susan Hruszowy, Merritt Gibson, Sherman Bleakney, Sherman Williams, Harold Forsythe, Bob Taylor, Rob Raeside, Andrew Hebda, Webster Andrews, and Ian McLaren, as well as Robin Anthony and Mary Kingston at Bowater Mersey. I am grateful to the others at the Nova Scotia Department of Natural Resources and the Nova Scotia Museum who offered their assistance along with the Central Nova Tourist Association and the Wolfville and Kentville branches of the Western Counties Regional Libraries.

Introduction

Comparable in size to Ireland, Nova Scotia is incomparable in so many ways. Much has been written about the province and its natural features. A geological history spanning more than 900 million years has given scientists plenty to puzzle.

Some of the most productive marine environments in the world are found in Nova Scotia and are supported by over 1 million km^2 (400,000 sq. mi.) of continental shelf and slope waters.

Changes to the shape and face of the province—sometimes subtle, sometimes dramatic—are always underway. A modified continental climate diffuses temperature extremes; however, the impact of the Atlantic Ocean on the province is often anything but moderate. Rock, sand, gravel, and mud shores are continuously eroded by tides and waves.

The Bay of Fundy tides, in particular, never fail to inspire awe. Ships that rest on the mud flats at low tide are buoyed to surprising heights—up to 16 m (45 ft.) if conditions are right. Nova Scotia is said to tilt slightly under the immense weight of 14 billion tonnes (more than 15 billion tons) of seawater as it flows into the Minas Basin twice daily.

Venturing deep into one of the province's lush old-growth forests or its spectacular highlands may be the only way to forget that the sea is never more than 56 km (35 mi.) away. Nova Scotia's diverse and dramatic 8,050 km (5,000 mi.) of coastline is like a jewel necklace. From soft white sand to sea-polished basalt shorelines to breathtaking sea cliffs towering far above the shore, Nova Scotia beaches, parks, and natural sites offer unique opportunities for memorable adventure and enjoyment.

The ocean-rimmed land mass supports a variety of flora and fauna. At Kentville Ravine, for example, visitors will find a surprising array of striking fungi and more species of rhododendrons than one might imagine. Natural havens may be found in the heart of busy towns like Truro's sprawling Victoria Park, complete with waterfalls, or Halifax's woodland Point Pleasant Park. Beautiful Melmerby Beach on the Sunrise Trail has all the facilities for a fun family outing. Gangly massive moose and Canada lynx find refuge in the boreal highlands of Cape Breton Island. Taylor Head Provincial Park along the Marine Drive offers scenic hiking trails and a gorgeous beach. At Kejimkujik National Park, campers can canoe on tranquil waters or enjoy a guided nature hike.

The Nova Scotia Department of Environment oversees approximately 12,500 ha (30,873 acres) of operational parkland; 17,200 ha (42,536 acres) of non-operational parkland and 1,100 km (684 mi.) of abandoned rail corridor. This department is also responsible for 91 designated beaches protected under the Beaches Act, 7 nature reserves designated under the Special Places Protection Act, and 31 candidate protected areas incorporating almost 300,000 ha (or 719,000 acres). Nonetheless, access has never been better. Over half of our provincial parks offer facilities for people who are physically challenged. Visitors from abroad, especially from countries where space is at a premium, are in awe of this province, where there is plenty of "elbow room" for everyone. Nova Scotians find their ties renewed in rediscovering their home province.

According to *The Natural History of Nova Scotia,* there is "a diversity of terrestrial landscape and habitat packed into about 55,000 sq km^2 (21,000 sq mi.) which is not found in many areas of comparable size in Canada." Exploring such a vast territory in one fell swoop may not be feasible for most of us, but enjoying the places to which we do travel is as sure as the rhythm of the tides.

Note: Some sites include maps that are from various sources and therefore not of a consistent scale. Maps to scale include: the Scenic Travelways Map (scale: 1:64,000), available from Visitor Information Centres around the province; *Map of the Province of Nova Scotia* (scale 1:250,000) available in bookstores; and topographical maps (scales 1:50,000 and 1:250,000), available from the Government Bookstore.

Symbols

- Washrooms
- Wheelchair accessible
- Parking
- Food
- Disposal station
- Picnic tables
- Admission
- Outdoor fireplace
- Fire wood supplied (campgrounds)
- Information (visitor information centre)
- National park or museum
- Provincial Park
- Pit toilets
- Toilet, sink, and/or shower
- Swimming
- Change houses
- Viewpoints/Observation decks
- Hiking
- Camping

Evangeline Trail

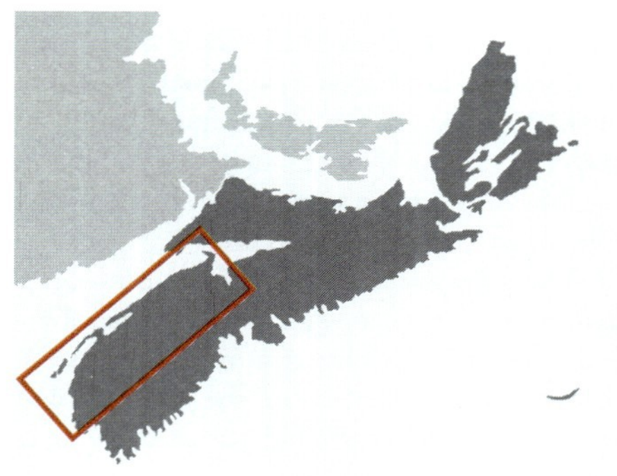

1 Ellenwood Lake Provincial Park
2 Chebogue Meadows
3 Mavillette Beach Provincial Park
4 Smugglers Cove Provincial Park
5 Mickey Hill Pocket Wilderness
6 Digby Neck/Long Island
7 Brier Island
8 Delap's Cove Wilderness Trail System
9 Grand Pré Dykelands
10 Evangeline Beach
11 Kentville Ravine
12 Hall's Harbour
13 Blomidon Provincial Park
14 Kings County Look-Off

1

Ellenwood Lake Provincial Park

Although surrounded by the sea, Nova Scotia's abundant freshwater habitats should not be overlooked. Lakes, streams, and bogs are examples of effects of the glaciers, which, fifteen thousand years ago, deposited eroded materials that blocked the flow of rivers and streams, creating lakes such as Ellenwood.

The water of Ellenwood Lake, in the heart of Yarmouth County, travels through a maze of bogs and woodlands, soaking up humic materials along the inevitable journey toward the sea. Lakes with water of a hue that resembles tea are common in Nova Scotia.

Snowshoeing around Ellenwood Lake is a great way to exercise the mind and the body. The winter scenery is striking in this tranquil setting.

Healthy populations of brown and speckled trout, chain pickerel, yellow and white perch, and Atlantic salmon draw fishing enthusiasts to the lush inland lake environment at Ellenwood.

The infrequent orchid *Platanthera flava* is a highlight when nature walks are led through the area. Plant life also includes cattail and pickerel-weed near the banks and floating species such as yellow pond lily farther from shore. Milfoil, pond weeds, and stonewort—a type of freshwater alga—thrive in the shallows. These vegetation zones in turn provide a habitat for worms, snails, clams, and insects such as the showy and acrobatic dragonfly.

Among the rich bird life in the park, look for the common loon (an excellent swimmer and diver), the red-tailed hawk, the American kestrel, and the barred owl, which are all quite common. The haunting call of the loon epitomizes the summertime lakeside experience.

The lush hardwood forests for which this park is known make a beautiful backdrop for wintertime activities such as cross-country skiing, tobogganing, skating, and snowshoeing.

Park facilities include a playground, a boat launch, and supervised swimming.

Directions: From Yarmouth, take Exit 34 off Highway 101. Proceed 6.5 km (4.1 mi.) along Route 340 and follow the signs to the Ellenwood Lake park entrance. The park is located approximately 19 km (12 mi.) northeast of Yarmouth.

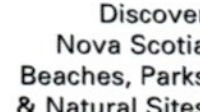

Chebogue Meadows

2

The interpretive trail at Chebogue Meadows was designed to preserve and showcase a representative group of wildlife habitats in the province's southwest interior. The provincially run nature site is located near some of the best salt-marshes on Nova Scotia's Atlantic coast. Along the Chebogue River and at Pinkneys Point, interpretive stations highlight distinct wildlife habitats: dry barrens; bog; black spruce swamp; maple-alder floodplain; stream; meadow; softwood forest; maple swamp; hardwood hill; cut-over; red spruce forest; and wetlands.

Bird life thrives in the woodlands with good cover and ample food supply.

For most of the year, the 4.5 km (2.8 mi.) trail is wet or damp, so appropriate footwear is a good idea. A leisurely pace will take visitors around the trail in roughly an hour and a half. The small stream that meanders through the meadow and eventually becomes the Chebogue River is important to wildlife along its entire length.

Chebogue Meadows hosts a variety of wildlife habitats, including salt-marshes.

Beaver, muskrat, mink, or raccoons may be seen feeding in or near the water. Kingfishers enjoy the abundant fish and swallows feed on the rich insect supply.

Wood ticks, probably introduced into the province by dogs from the U. S. about the turn of the century, are present in southwestern Nova Scotia in early summer.

In *A Naturalist's Notebook*, author Charles Allen describes a marsh at this site: "A great flock of Starlings, like a plume of smoke in the distance, wheels and dips over the Chebogue marshes, changing shape by the moment: now a sphere, then a lens, an hour glass, breaking in two and rejoining before finally fading into the haze." Such scenes can still be enjoyed here.

Directions: From Yarmouth, follow Highway 340 toward Corberrie for about 6 km (4 mi.). Watch for signs announcing the park.

P

3 Mavillette Beach Provincial Park

The strip of coastline along the St. Mary's Bay known as the French Shore is more widely known for its Acadian and fishing heritage than for recreational beaches, but the provincial park at Mavillette Beach, with its large fertile salt-marsh and sizeable sand dunes, is well worth a visit.

Located just south of Cape St. Marys, Mavillette is a small Acadian community, well-loved by local residents. At the local beach, the temperature of the water may keep swimming to a minimum except on the hottest days, but people flock here just the same to soak up the sun and stroll along the scenic shoreline.

At one time, the sand dunes here were used for recreation, considered ideal for climbing, sliding, and digging. Dune buggies and four-wheelers were a common sight. These days, the dunes' fragility has eclipsed such self-indulgent pursuits in exchange for concentrated efforts toward their protection.

Gulls hover over Mavillette Beach in search of food.

Wooden boardwalks have been built to help protect the delicate sand dune ecosystem, bound only by thin soil and a network of plant roots.

Dunes, found in areas where beach sand is plentiful from eroding headlands and drumlins, are accumulated as strong wave action and wind pile the sand into ridges, or berms, at the top of a beach.

There are about 250 species of shells to be found in local waters; some can be washed up on this shore.

Directions: From Yarmouth head north on Route 1 towards Mavillette Beach. Turn left at John Doucette Road, which leads to the park.

Smugglers Cove Provincial Park

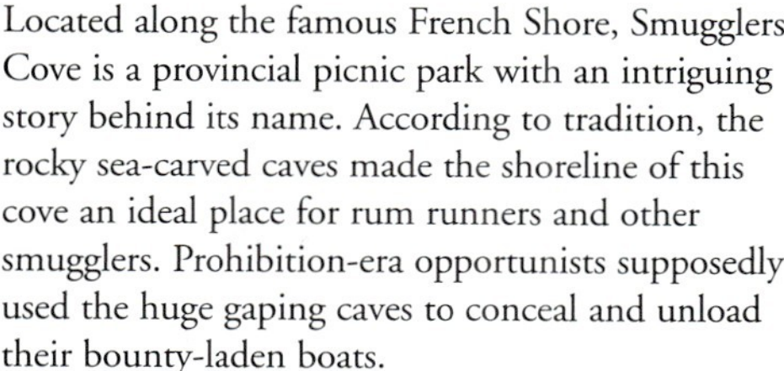

Located along the famous French Shore, Smugglers Cove is a provincial picnic park with an intriguing story behind its name. According to tradition, the rocky sea-carved caves made the shoreline of this cove an ideal place for rum runners and other smugglers. Prohibition-era opportunists supposedly used the huge gaping caves to conceal and unload their bounty-laden boats.

The Smugglers Cove Provincial Park is a picturesque spot to lay out a picnic lunch, where visitors can safely lounge, perched atop the rocky cliffs overlooking St. Mary's Bay. Energetic folk can tackle the steep wooden stairway down to the pebble beach. A separate short flight of stairs leads to a fenced-in viewpoint for a better look at the cliffs, sea caves, and beach far below.

On a foggy day, it is especially easy to see how this secluded cove would have appealed to early smugglers.

The park lies just south of Meteghan, the busiest fishing port along the Acadian shore that hugs St. Mary's Bay. Called "la Ville Française" (French Town) by older generations, a dozen or so French-speaking communities are knit closely together along a 40 km (25 mi.) stretch of the province's southwestern shore.

Many residents are descended from among the first European settlers to come from France after 1632. According to oral tradition, Acadians who escaped the deportation order first appeared in this region about 1755–1756.

Today, manicured homes, elegant churches, seafood restaurants, antique and craft shops, service stations, inns, and food markets are familiar sights on the stretch of highway along the French Shore, known as North America's longest main street.

Directions: From Yarmouth, head north toward Digby on Route 1. Continue straight past Mavillette Beach. Smugglers Cove is on the left just before Meteghan.

5 Mickey Hill Pocket Wilderness

Mickey Hill Pocket Wilderness is owned and well maintained by the Liverpool-based Bowater Mersey Paper Company Ltd. With the exception of some steep staircases (which can be avoided) the gravelled trails and boardwalks over rough terrain make the walking easy and maintain the character of this marvellous woodland spot.

On a walk through these woods, the path is strewn in places with rocks and roots—caution is recommended—but it leads to an inviting sandy beach at Lamb Lake (a lovely spot for swimming) and to the shores of the lively and picturesque Allains River. Marshes rich with native sedge, grasses, and wild iris flourish near the river's edge.

The red squirrel thrives in the tranquil Mickey Hill Pocket Wilderness.

The pocket wilderness is peppered with rocks and boulders of various sizes, known as erratics. The location of these rocks tells geologists a great deal about how glaciers moved. Mosses, lichen, and ferns grow like garnishes on these rock surfaces now.

Pileated woodpeckers can be spied in these woods. Shy creatures, they avoid open woodland near habitations. Unlike other woodpecker species, this one square-cuts the entrance to its nest and often excavates for food with square corners, too. The great horned owl finds shelter among the yellow birch, maple, poplar, oak, white pine, hemlock, and red spruce.

After exploring the wooded path, a dip in Lamb Lake is a refreshing escape from the summer heat.

Twinflower thrives in cool mossy woodlands, wooded swamps, and spruce bogs. The mayflower, Nova Scotia's official flower, the bluebead lily, and the showy—and endangered—Lady's-slipper share the area with red and flying squirrels, chipmunks, raccoons, and porcupines.

The site is open year-round so cross-country skiers and snowshoe enthusiasts can enjoy the scenery when it is cloaked in new-fallen snow.

Directions: From Annapolis Royal take Route 8 south for about 10 km (6 mi.). (Route 8 is Kejimkujik Scenic Drive and joins the Annapolis Valley to the South Shore near Milton.) Do not take the Mickey Hill trunk road on the right-hand side of the highway. A little further ahead on the left is a large sign for the pocket wilderness.

🚻 P

Digby Neck/Long Island

People tend to rush past this slim strip of basalt which separates the Bay of Fundy from St. Mary's Bay on their way to Brier Island, but there is much worth exploring along the Digby Neck and Islands Scenic Drive. Also known as Route 217, the road shoots straight down the narrow peninsula, breaking for brief ferry rides at East Ferry and Freeport.

Whale- and seabird-watching tours are popular off Digby Neck and Long Island.

Digby Neck and Long Island are part of the southwest end of North Mountain, a long basalt ridge. This ridge is home to species of rare and Threatened Atlantic coastal plain flora. Southwestern Nova Scotia is the only region in Canada where the *Lophiola aurea,* or Golden Crest is found. This and other rare plants are the big concern of various groups, including the Society for the Preservation of Eastern Head, a local organization dedicated to protecting sensitive ecology.

The rich marine ecosystem surrounding Digby Neck and Long Island has piqued the interest of scientists and tourists. The sense of wonder that accompanies whale, seabird, and seal sightings has nurtured the growing appeal of "watching" tours.

The Balancing Rock near Tiverton shows how, over eons, molten lava can become a gravity-defying formation.

Marine influences are everywhere. Fishing villages sport wharves piled with nets and lobster traps. Beaches and coves strewn with storm-borne driftwood and other flotsam and jetsam are favourite stopping spots.

Long Island's Museum and Tourist Bureau in the village of Tiverton has exhibits highlighting local history and details on where to eat and stay. Inquire here for information on guided whale- and seabird-watching tours, deep sea fishing, and nature tours. Call (902)839-2853.

Near Tiverton, on Long Island, there is a hiking trail that leads to the famous Balancing Rock. The tall, slim, precariously perched formation has become one of the area's most celebrated features and deserves its reputation as a geological oddity.

Directions: From Digby, take Route 217. The ferry between East Ferry and Tiverton leaves every hour on the half-hour. Cars cost one dollar for a round trip; pedestrians ride free.

7

Brier Island

Recently, Brier Island has become synonymous with whale watching, but those with a passion for botany know the place as a rich source of intriguing plants like Eastern Mountain Avens (*Geum peckii*), an herbaceous perennial at least 46 cm (18 in.) high with yellow flowers that are similar to the common buttercup. In botanical circles, this rare native plant is the toast of the island, and well it should be—Eastern Mountain Avens is known to grow in only three places in the world: on mountaintops in New Hampshire, on Brier Island, and on Digby Neck.

One of the most spectacular sights to behold off Brier Island is a whale breaching the Fundy waters.

Other noteworthy plants found on Brier Island include the curly-grass fern—said to be unlike any other fern in appearance—and the relatively rare knee-high dwarf birch found only in a few places in the province. A portion of Brier Island was recently declared a protected site because of its delicate ecology.

The fragile little harebells clinging to soil-thin crevices are the best reminders of the island's vulnerability to the Bay of Fundy tides and winter weather. In the winter, storms sweep the tiny island with a vengeance; although in summer the climate can be idyllic.

Three lighthouses are a testament to the sometimes hazardous sailing conditions which have littered the shoals with shipwrecks. Look for the Westport monument to Joshua Slocum, a native son who was the first person to circumnavigate the globe. He disappeared at sea sometime after November 1909.

The Bay of Fundy surrounding Brier Island and adjacent Long Island has long teemed with fish in seemingly endless abundance. Although stocks have markedly declined, lobster, cod, pollock, herring, hake, and haddock still support a fishing economy.

The rich marine habitat encourages whale-watching tours, which draw scores of visitors to the island annually. On any given day, humpbacks, minkes, harbour porpoises, and white-sided dolphins may be spotted. Pilot whales, white-beaked dolphins, and the rare Northern right whale make

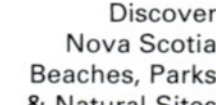

less frequent appearances.

The abundant food supply also attracts seals. In northern areas of the island, grey and harbour seals lumber onto beaches. They are especially common at Seal Cove.

Ornithologists are drawn to the island for its varied bird life and its status as an important staging area for the fall and spring migration of songbirds and hawks. Black-headed gulls; roseate, common tern and Arctic tern; common eider; great and double-crested cormorant; Bonaparte's gull; sandpiper; plover; shearwater; and other seabirds and waterfowl can be seen by bird watchers and photographers. In the fall, tens of thousands of migrating phalarope feast on a smorgasbord of marine nutrients, such as copepods and krill, that are borne to the sea's surface by upwellings.

Dramatic rugged cliffs around Brier Island overlook the Bay of Fundy. Visitors may spot the varied marine wildlife from land.

Though small in size (6 km or 4 mi. long and 2 km and 1.5 mi. wide), Brier Island is big on recreational opportunities, including bird watching, nature photography, deep sea fishing, whale-watching and seabird tours, beachcombing, and rockhounding. Informative guided nature tours are also available. Trails are user-friendly for all ages and fitness levels.

With frequent ferry runs, the island is accessible by car and on foot. Dining, accommodations, gift shops, groceries, fuel, and a Visitors Information Centre are located on the island.

Directions: From Digby take the Digby Neck and Islands Scenic Drive (Route 217) to East Ferry at the end of Digby Neck, then board the ferry to Tiverton, Long Island. Continue southwest toward Freeport, where another ferry carries passengers to Westport, Brier Island. Both ferry rides are short and service operates hourly (weather permitting), twenty-four hours a day. One dollar round trip for cars; no charge for passengers.

8

Delap's Cove Wilderness Trail

Exploring the Delap's Cove Wilderness Trail System is an adventure in the southwestern end of the Annapolis Valley along the 10 km (6 mi.) trail system. Two connected loops on 52.5 ha (130 acres) border the Bay of Fundy.

Bohaker Trail loops for about 2 km (1 mi.) beginning near the parking area. The trail starts across a low escarpment overlooking the Bay of Fundy then winds through a fern-filled forest before stretching along the shoreline. Dense stands of pine and spruce mark the end of the trail. A observation deck along the way gives a bird's-eye view of the 13 m (43 ft.) Bohaker Falls and a small cliff-lined cove cluttered with driftwood.

Roughly a forty-five-minute hike up an old logging road leads to the wilder-looking and rougher Charlie's Trail, about a 2 km (1 mi.) loop that has a number of access points to the Bay of Fundy beach. Delicate goldenthread, a buttercup relative with five white petals, still grows here.

A variety of plants at Delap's Cove were once used for medicinal purposes by early inhabitants.

Side paths off the loops include one that leads to a secluded spot on Charlie's Brook and another is fringed with fragrant bayberry shrubs. A traipse to the shore reveals basalt formations, edible sea lettuce and dulse, mussels, periwinkles, and barnacles.

Directions: From Annapolis Royal, proceed east on Highway 1 to Parker Mountain Road. Turn left and proceed to Parker's Cove. Turn left and follow the Shore Road to the community of Delap's Cove. Signs direct visitors to the trail. Or head east to the turn off for the Port Royal Habitation and continue west on Victoria Beach Road. Turn right onto Hollow Mountain Road (unpaved). Proceed to Delap's Cove then follow the signs to the trail.

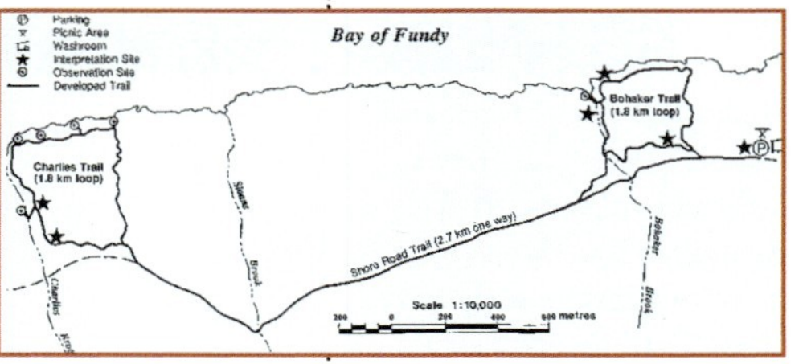

Grand Pré Dykelands

9

Acadians brought their farming and dyke building skills to the Minas Basin region in the 1680s. It was the most heavily populated area in the French colony of Acadia, until the British began deporting the Acadians in 1755 for refusing to take the Oath of Allegiance to the British crown.

Dyking converted the abundant tidal marshes of the area to useful agricultural land, but reclaiming marshlands required Herculean endurance and patience as rectangular sods were cut and piled to form a tall, tapering mound. Dykes aided farming and settlement in the vicinity not only of Grand Pré but also Wolfville, Port Williams, and Canard. With dyking, more than 85 per cent of the Bay of Fundy's salt-marshes have been converted to agricultural land.

Gazing over the area, it's easy to see why the Acadians bestowed the name "Grand Pré," meaning "great meadow." The dykelands surrounding Grand Pré National Historic Site have since evolved into a delicate ecosystem rich in wildlife.

This terrain is home to muskrat, mice, and mink and the birds that prey upon them: short-eared owls, Northern harriers, American kestrels, red-tailed hawks and an occasional gyrfalcon in winter. Watch for raptors perched on fence posts or the tops of power poles and wires. In October, rough-legged hawks from the Arctic scan the landscape for rodents.

Shorebirds flee the beaches and roost in the dykelands when the tide is high. Grand Pré and other dykelands are favoured grazing grounds for migrant flocks of Canada Geese. Great black-headed, ring-billed, and herring gulls join crows and ravens to feast on fields spread with barn scraps doubling as fertilizer. Dyked grasslands hold possibilities for fall sightings of four common songbirds from the Arctic: horned lark, American pipit, Lapland longspur, and snow bunting.

The dykelands at Grand Pré were created by the Acadians more than three centuries ago to enhance the soil's fertility for agriculture.

Maintained by the Nova Scotia Department of Agriculture and Marketing, the Grand Pré dykelands are "3,013 acres (of land) below sea level behind 28,455 feet of dyke," according to a roadside sign.

As part of the National Historic Site, there is a small memorial church with artwork depicting the Acadian life and Deportation. Also on display are artifacts from early Acadian households. Of course, here stands the bronze statue of Evangeline, based on Longfellow's poem of the same title, amid aged trees and colourful flower beds in bloom during the summer. The memorial site overlooks the dykelands.

Directions: From Wolfville, take Highway 1 east then turn left at the Grand Pré National Historic Site sign. The park is a short drive from the turn. Parking is clearly marked on the right. Services are available in season at the National Historic Site office and gift shop.

Evangeline Beach

Against the striking backdrop of a Nova Scotia landmark—Blomidon—Evangeline Beach can become rowdy with the cacophony raised by hundreds of thousands of migratory shorebirds from mid-July to mid-September. They leave their Arctic breeding grounds and congregate along the intertidal mud flats of the Minas Basin.

Mud flats at Evangeline Beach, nearby Avonport Beach, and the Windsor Causeway, are migratory hot spots because these areas support a teeming population of small marine life, including clams, worms, and mud shrimp, which lure more than twenty species of shorebirds like kids to a candy store. The main food source, the burrowing amphipod *Corophium volutator* (mud shrimp), occurs in North America only in intertidal mud flats of the Bay of Fundy and the Gulf of Maine. The best time to observe shorebirds is one to two hours before and after high tide when they congregate. There are no comparable feeding grounds farther south on the Atlantic seaboard in late summer.

Migratory shorebirds flock to Evangeline Beach to feed on the food-rich intertidal flats.

The tiny semipalmated sandpiper, which predominates the beach, along with black-bellied and semipalmated plover, Hudsonian godwit, dowitcher, greater and lesser yellowleg, ruddy turnstone, sanderling, dunlin, and least and white-rumped sandpiper stalk the intertidal zone (the area between high tide and low tide), feeding on invertebrates burrowed in the mud.

The mud flats not only provide a rich marine habitat, they're great fun for visitors with a yen for mudlarking or scrounging for unusual debris. Most people find footwear a hindrance on the mud flats because the sticky ooze clings to shoes. Those with a sense of adventure enjoy mud sliding during the incoming tide, but caution is required to avoid sharp objects and mollusc shells.

Directions: From Wolfville, head east on Highway 1. Turn left at the Grand Pré National Historic Site sign and continue past the historic site, on the Grand Pré Road, to the beach.

11

Kentville Ravine

One of the last remaining old-growth Eastern hemlock forests (more than 250 years old) in Nova Scotia lies just a short jaunt from downtown Kentville. By the early 1960s preservation of the ravine was decided upon. Today, joggers, walkers, and cross-country skiers of all levels of fitness enjoy the park year-round.

Kentville Ravine offers woodland paths that run along a brook, and wind toward a waterfall.

The ravine trail begins near the entrance to the Kentville Agricultural Centre, a facility for provincial and federal research. Park in the gravel lot then cross toward the fence and head left on the gravel path. The trail slices through an open area before leading into the still and dusky forest habitat where roughly 125 species of flowering plants, including Jack-in-the-pulpit and some rare orchids, thrive under the canopy. Elderkin Brook, which runs northward along the floor of the ravine and empties into the Cornwallis River, is a constant companion as hikers make their way toward the waterfall at the end of the trail.

As the trail winds up and out of the ravine on the approach to the waterfall, watch out for very steep drop-offs. There are no guard rails and footing can be slippery near the edge.

The ravine is a rich and important fungal site. For at least the last fifty years it has been one of the major sources in Nova Scotia for mushrooms used for scientific record. The highly diversified fungal flora consists of some of the most spectacular fungi in the province, from the extremely poisonous *Amanita virosa* to some of the smallest and most beautiful mycenas.

Diverse wildlife thrives in the forest cover here. Little Brown Bats, northern flying squirrels, ermine, mink, chipmunks, and smoky shrews find sanctuary. The pileated woodpecker, magnolia warbler, gray catbird, song sparrow, and black-capped chickadee are just a few of the bird species that enliven this landscape that seems worlds away from city life.

Directions: The gravel parking lot for Kentville Ravine is located at the east end of Kentville on Highway 1. From the parking area, cross a grassy patch toward the fence and head left on the gravel path that starts amid the trees.

P

Hall's Harbour

Hall's Harbour is postcard-perfect and endlessly photographed. When summer shrouds the Annapolis Valley in a veil of heat and humidity, residents head here for respite and, perhaps, a fresh lobster supper overlooking the shore. Now a haven for tourists and summer residents, the village once thrived on the fishing industry. Weirs dotted the shore, and community suppers were feasts of salmon and lobster.

Hall's Harbour reflects its fishing heritage in the sights around the picturesque village.

Individuals and community groups work to keep the gravel and stone beach at Hall's Harbour clean in spite of the dramatic Fundy tides. Flanked by steep basalt cliffs capped with groves of hardwoods and softwoods, the rugged beach terrain is ideal for explorers of all ages. Children especially love poking around the curious little cubbyholes and dark, tiny caves along the shore. Driftwood, shells, and minerals such as agate, quartz, zeolites, and amethyst are treasures waiting to be found.

An old fish house dating back to 1885 accommodates the Hall's Harbour Museum and Interpretive Centre, where artifacts evoke the days when fishing, lumber, and sailing ships defined local culture. Eco-trails meander through the woods on the east and west sides of the village. Reconstruction of the old Lighthouse Wharf with a wheelchair accessible walkway is part of a project started in the fall of 1997 by the federal government's Katimavik Program and the Hall's Harbour Community Development Association.

Some people come to Hall's Harbour simply to drink in the view. Across the Minas Channel are the cliffs and lighthouse of Cape d'Or and Cape Chignecto, while the unmistakable jagged silhouette of Cape Split appears to the right in the distance.

Directions: From Kentville, follow Route 359 straight to Hall's Harbour, a ten- to fifteen-minute drive.

Evangeline Trail

13

Blomidon Provincial Park

A breathtaking blend of farm fields and coastal scenes greets travellers as they approach one of Nova Scotia's most famous and distinctive landmarks: 750 ha (1,875 acres) of park land blanketing a large portion of the spectacular promontory known as Cape Blomidon.

The park is one of the province's most visited natural sites. From the time it opens in mid-June until closing in mid-October, the park entices thousands of visitors for its varied landscapes and habitats, spectacular geological features, abundant wildlife, and recreational opportunities. Hikers enjoy a 14 km (8.5 mi.) system of interconnected hiking trails with striking views overlooking the Bay of Fundy and an unsupervised beach.

The view from Cape Blomidon overlooks the area of the world's highest tides. Nearby Cape Split, pictured here, is subjected to the dramatic tides too, from its position in the Minas Basin.

The Mi'kmaq called Cape Blomidon *Owbogegechk,* meaning "abounding with dogwood." Europeans were less poetic; they dubbed it "blow-me-down" in recognition of the gusty winds. Natives honoured the region as the home of the great Glooscap, who, according to native tradition, pitched his wigwam and reigned as Lord of the Land of the Rising Sun amid the towering trees.

Cape Blomidon is part of the easternmost extension of North Mountain. The volcanic basalt that forms much of the mountain, stretching from Brier Island in the west to Cape Split in the east, forms a protective cap over softer sandstone and shale at the Cape. On a map, Blomidon and nearby Cape Split look like a jagged hook slicing into the Minas Basin.

Looking back at the red sandstone cliffs from any vantage point on the beach reveals clearly the powers of erosion. On the cliff tops, tree roots are exposed to the air.

The view from Cape Blomidon overlooks the highest rise and fall of tides in the world. It's said that 14 billion tons of sea water surge into the Minas Basin twice daily. The force is equal to the flow of water produced by all the major rivers of the world combined! Because tides here move into

the basin so quickly—up to 15 km/hr (8–9 mi./hr) and reach far up onto cliff faces—coastline hikers are advised to be aware of the tide. (It can rise as much as 1 m or 3 ft. in only twenty minutes.) Low tide exposes an expanse of mud flats ripe for beachcombing.

Ambitious bird watchers can spot more than one hundred different species, including the rare peregrine falcon. Large flocks of shorebirds that flock to Cape Blomidon to feed on mud shrimp from July through August have earned the area a place in the Western Hemisphere Shorebird Reserve Network. Blackburnian and other warblers, hermit thrush, peewee, and red-eyed vireo are common as are cedar waxwing and the red-breasted nuthatch.

In late May, trillium, violets, Lady's-slippers, Dutchman's breeches and especially spring beauties carpet the forest floor. The rare wild leek pops up in lush patches in early spring but resists flowering until early summer when its leaves have disappeared.

Forests of sugar maple, yellow birch, beech, fir, red and white spruce, and mud flats, swamp, fen and bog are home to coyote, white-tailed deer, striped skunks, short-tailed weasels, snowshoe hare, red-backed voles, and porcupines. Harbour porpoises, Atlantic white-sided dolphins, and seals occasionally pursue a meal into the Minas Basin.

It's tough to find a more tranquil yet varied environment in which to wile away the day. Scenery and recreation, flora and fauna all await.

Directions: From Wolfville, take Highway 1 west then turn at the Port Williams intersection. Follow Route 358 to the village of Canning. Watch for the blue park sign on the right. Turn left and continue on Route 358 to Blomidon. To explore the lower beach, park at the entrance then follow the path through the picnic area, down some wooden stairs that lead to the beach. The coastal trail is accessible from the campground area in the upper park. Visitors will find a map of the trail system posted near the park entrance and maps along the trails.

14 Kings County Look-off

Look-offs like this one on the North Mountain (not a true mountain, but a long, low-lying ridge) above the Annapolis Valley, give visitors a breath-taking view. On a particularly clear day the vista embraces five counties. The town of Wolfville, roughly 18 km (11 mi.) away to the south, is part of the landscape.

From atop the Look-off, spectacular panoramas of the beautiful Minas Basin await.

The look-off is elevated above the Annapolis-Cornwallis Valley by Jurassic volcanic rocks, which proved harder and more resistant to erosion than underlying sandstone in the valley below.

The solidified basaltic lava flow, which towers more than 205 m (675 ft.) above the valley floor is 208 million years old. The lava burst forth when North America began to break away from Africa as the supercontinent Pangaea rifted apart.

On the opposite horizon, the skyline takes in South Upland, underlain by 370 million-year-old Devonian granites. To the left the Carboniferous lowlands of neighboring Hants County are backed by the harder slate-cored Rawdon Hills.

The view from the Kings County Look-off is one of the prettiest in the province. On a clear day, visitors can see three counties in Nova Scotia and two in New Brunswick from here.

Below the Look-off, low hills, bumps, and ridges (moraine deposits) caused by sand and gravel left by melting ice sheets add texture to the landscape. Valley farms with patchwork fields add colour to the spectacular view that rewards those who make their way up the steep North Mountain slope.

Extending from the eastern end of St. Mary's Bay in the west, to the mouth of the Cornwallis River in the east, the valley is renowned for its farmlands and apple orchards. The communities clustered along the shores of the Minas Basin, and further inland, share a heritage of shipbuilding, farming and fishing.

Directions: From Wolfville, head west on Route 1 about 5 km (3 mi.) Turn right at the Irving service station onto Route 358, heading north through Port Williams and further north through Canning. Turn left at the Soldier's Monument and proceed to the top of the mountain, bearing right. There is a privately run campground directly across from the look-off.

Glooscap Trail

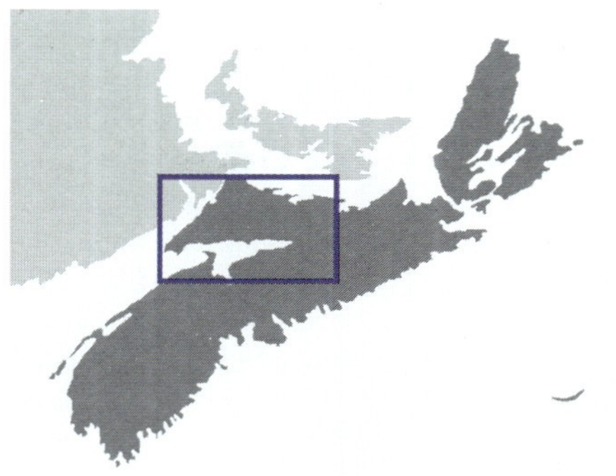

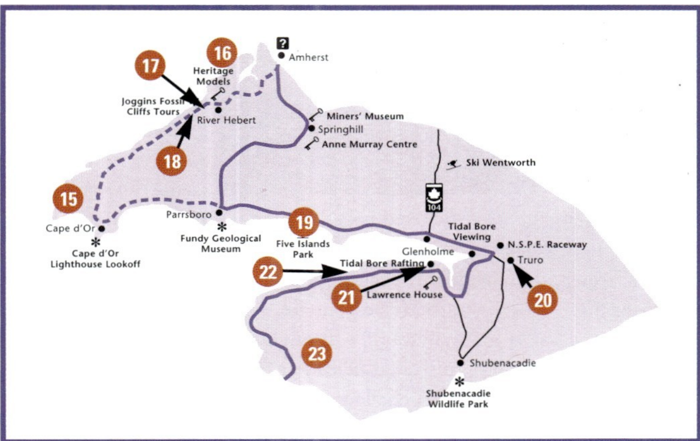

15 Cape Chignecto Provincial Park
16 Minudie Interpretive Park
17 River Hebert Tidal Bore Park
18 Joggins Fossil Cliffs
19 Five Islands Provincial Park
20 Victoria Park
21 Anthony Provincial Park
22 Burncoat Head Park
23 Smiley's Provincial Park

15 Cape Chignecto Provincial Park

The Cape Chignecto coastline is steeped in scenery so dramatic, it inspired an entire community to take part in the development and management of Nova Scotia's newest and largest provincial park. A long-time dream to preserve this diverse coastline wilderness will be realized when the park, which was developed as a partnership between the community and the provincial government, officially opens in early 1998. (Visitors have access prior to the official opening.)

Cape Chignecto Provincial Park, Nova Scotia's largest, overlooks the Chignecto and Minas Basins.

Located at the westernmost end of the Cobequid Mountains, the park covers 4,532 ha (11,200 acres) and is part of the Avalon ecozone. The highest cliffs in Nova Scotia (200 m or 656 ft.) dominate a landscape of beaches, sheltered coves, sea caves, and red spruce forests.

Plant life includes at least a dozen infrequent plant species, such as white snakeroot and creeping rattlesnake plantain. Moose and white-tailed deer may wander through hardwood stands and cultivated fields left from early settlements.

A challenging 30–40 km (19 to 25 mi.) hiking trail will be the crowning attraction. The trail begins at Red Rocks, a geological point of interest as a major fault line. When completed, the trail will lead upward to an elevation of 75 m (246 ft.) before levelling off to continue toward the coast, across hardwood ridges and into steep valleys. Hikers will be able to explore the beach and enjoy spectacular views of the Minas and Chignecto Basins.

The park is fully serviced for day-users to back country campers.

Directions: From Amherst follow Route 2. Turn right onto Route 302. Turn right again onto Route 242 toward River Hebert and Apple River. The provincial park is located on the north side of the Minas Basin, approximately 5 km (3 mi.) west of Advocate Harbour and 11 km (6.5 mi.) southwest of Apple River.

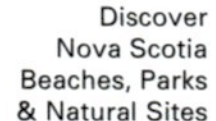

Minudie Interpretive Park

16

The peace and quiet which typifies Minudie today is far different from the days when agriculture and coal mines, sandstone quarries and logging operations thrived. The fascinating natural history of the area is highlighted by a series of interpretive panels. Created at the mouth of River Hebert, the park overlooks the immense tidal landscape strung with sturdy dykes.

The Minudie interpretive park overlooks the Elysian Fields where the Acadians built dykes to gain fertile farmland.

Stretching north from the village of Minudie, where early Acadians settled, is a vast open area of dykeland known as the Elysian Fields, roughly 1,200 ha (3,000 acres) of which are used today for pasturing cattle and growing crop hay. In the Acadian dyke system, drainage ditches combined with an ingenious one-way water gate called an *aboiteau* allowed fresh water to run off the marshes at low tide but kept salt water from flowing onto the fields as the tide rolled in.

Amos (King) Seaman, left his mark on the area. By the mid-1800s, grindstones were being shipped worldwide annually from the Seaman quarry. A cairn at the interpretive park honours Seaman's memory, along with the Catholic and Universalist churches that he built (open to visitors daily) and the school he created, which is now an artifact-filled museum.

In the northern reaches of Chignecto Bay, Minudie is part of the Tantramar Eco-zone, famous for its salt-marshes and migratory birds. The thousands of migrating waterfowl, which descend on the Tantramar annually from August to December, inspired the Acadians to call the region *Tintamarre,* meaning "din" or "racket."

Directions: Follow Route 2 from Amherst then turn right onto Route 302. Make another right turn on Route 242 to River Hebert, then right again to the Minudie turn-off.

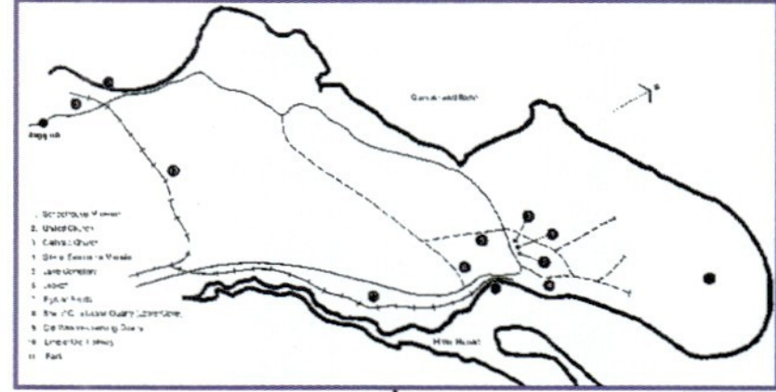

P

17 River Hebert Tidal Bore Park

At River Hebert, approximately 5 km (3 mi.) inland from the shores of Chignecto Bay, marshlands have played a key role in the construction of Atlantic Canada's first natural wetland sewage treatment system, a joint project involving Ducks Unlimited Canada, the community of River Hebert, and others. Nutrient-rich community wastewater feeds wetland plants such as cattails, sedges, and pond weed which, in turn, support a wide range of microscopic organisms that feed snails, insects, and other invertebrates. As a result, fish and waterfowl thrive in the enriched wetland.

The River Hebert Marsh can be explored as part of a walkabout that includes the Tidal Bore Park, the Heritage Models Centre, and the Miner's Museum. River Hebert is known as one of Nova Scotia's prime sites for tidal bore watching. When the incoming tide meets the outward flow of the river, the ensuing collision causes a rare phenomena called a tidal bore. The park has paved walkways, benches, and a dyke walk with magnificent viewing areas where visitors can get a bird's-eye view of the tidal bore. Watch for blue heron in the shallow water at low tide.

River Hebert Marsh is a scenic spot to watch the tidal bore roll in.

The Heritage Models Centre, billed as "a first class example of Canadian folk art at its best," houses realistic one-twelfth-scale copies of former and present buildings from the surrounding area. Folk artist Bud Johnston created these intricate works in his backyard.

At the Miner's Museum artifacts and photos recall an era when more than seventy mines were in operation in the surrounding area. A railway was built to carry coal to the Maccan power plant. The mines now lay fallow, but new uses are under exploration. One idea is to tap the geothermal energy from underground aquifers.

Directions: From Amherst, take Route 2 then turn right on Route 302. Make another right onto Route 242. Follow the Eco-tour signs to River Hebert. The Tidal Bore Park is located at the bridge near the entrance to the village.

Joggins Fossil Cliffs

The fossil cliffs at Joggins, a small village located on the northeastern shore of Chignecto Bay, is a worthwhile destination for any traveller with an interest in fossils and geology.

Some of the first land animals on earth have resurfaced at Joggins as fossilized remains. Fossilized tree roots, bark, leaves, and fern fronds are routinely discovered lying loose on the Joggins beach, and fossils of prehistoric plants, trees, and animal life are clearly visible along the renowned cliffs.

The area first became famous in the late 1840s, when its status was established as the world's best continuously exposed section of Late Carboniferous Period rocks (300 million years old). A decade later, excitement resurfaced when paleontology pioneers, Sir William Dawson and Sir Charles Lyell (friend and colleague of Sir Charles Darwin), discovered fossils of amphibians and some of the very first reptiles to have lived on earth.

Fossils at Joggins date back to the Late Carboniferous Period, 300 million years ago. These traces of ancient plant and animal life hold fascinating stories in their detail.

Three hundred million years ago, Arthropleura, a strange-looking arthropod resembling a giant sowbug, roamed the land that was also inhabited by salamander-like amphibians and lizardlike reptiles. All were ancestors of the dinosaurs that later came to dominate the earth for about 160 million years, until their own extinction about 65 million years ago. Visitors to Joggins may find fossilized tracks of Arthropleura, which grew up to 2 m (7 ft.) long and 30 cm (12 in.) wide. Tracks have been found in many places from the parking lot area to Lower Cove at the north end.

For geologists, the distinctive layers of coal in the cliffs tell a story of a completely different landscape with river systems and junglelike forests that were common during the Carboniferous Period. Most of the coal beds in North America were created about 360 million years ago, during the Late Carboniferous Period. The Joggins beds exposed in the cliffs were laid down about 300 million years ago.

To conserve important fossils for scientific research, the Joggins Fossil Cliffs have been designated a

P

Protected Site under the Special Places Protection Act. Before the site was protected by legislation, overzealous fossil hunters used dynamite and backhoes. Now a Heritage Research Permit from the Nova Scotia Museum is required to dig or remove fossils from the cliffs or reefs; however, visitors can freely gather the loose fossils on the beach.

Be wary of rock falls (avoid overhanging sections) and be sure to consult tide tables. The tides in the Bay of Fundy are fast and high.

Exploring along the Bay of Fundy at Joggins reveals fossils on the cliff faces. People of all ages enjoy the adventure.

The Joggins Fossil Centre, for which admission is charged, is a good place to begin and end a tour of the area. Staff at the centre will advise visitors where to hunt and what to expect to find. Puzzling discoveries on the beach can be brought back to the centre for free identification. The centre is open from June to the end of September, seven days a week. A gift shop has fossils, minerals, and souvenirs for sale. For further information call (902) 251-2727

Directions: From Amherst, take Route 2, turn right onto Route 302, and right again onto Route 242 to River Hebert. Follow the Glooscap Trail to Joggins.

Five Islands Provincial Park

19

According to the Mi'kmaq legend the area that is now Five Islands Provincial Park originated with Glooscap. He tore up huge fistfuls of land and hurled them at Beaver, with whom he was furious for spoiling his garden of healing medicines. These clumps of earth are said to be the five offshore basalt islands for which the park is named. The islands are called Moose, Diamond, Long, Egg, and Pinnacle.

The five islands are reminders of volcanic action, massive erosion, and glacial scouring that left a landscape prime for archeological discovery. Basalt formations cradle an abundance of semi-precious rocks and minerals such as agate and copper, but their removal is prohibited.

Unusual geological formations line the shore at Five Islands Provincial Park.

Five Islands belongs to an environmental region known as the Basalt Headlands Eco-zone, one of seventy-seven separate landscapes identified in Nova Scotia and detailed in the marvellous *Fundy Shore Eco-Guide* (see Sources). The volcanic outcroppings which blanket red Triassic sandstone were formed over 225 million years ago. Vast mud flats that characterize much of the Minas Basin are the result of millions of tonnes of sandstone eroding into the bay each year.

The infertile-looking intertidal flats actually teem with life. Under a cover of mud, minute inhabitants coexist: mud shrimp (*Corophium volutator*) in unimaginable numbers (up to 20,000 per m^2 of mud), the tiny clam *Macoma,* bigger soft-shelled clams, *Mya arenaria,* saltwater worms and other bottom-dwelling invertebrates. Semipalmated sandpiper (affectionately called "peeps"), greater yellowleg, and black-bellied plover feed upon this smorgasbord, as do raccoons, which skitter down from the woods above.

Five Islands clam flats represent a half-million dollar industry for the hardy souls who brave the gluelike mud and back-aching work. Low tide is

the time to gather the shad and flounder that have been caught in the weirs.

Above the flats, a different world exists. White spruce, balsam fir, red maple, and white birch are cover for deer, coyote, bear, porcupines, woodchucks, and other small mammals such as the short-tailed shrew and meadow vole. Birdsong from warbler, kinglet, siskin, and crossbill fills the forest. Moose Island is a bald eagle nesting site.

More than 13 km (8 mi.) of scenic walking trails traverse the 413 ha (1,020 acre) park. The 5 km (3 mi.) Red Head Trail skirts the 90 m (300 ft.) sea cliffs. Constant erosion make cliff edges precarious. Viewing areas have been established so visitors can safely enjoy the scenery. The park has an unsupervised beach.

Hikers enjoy panoramic views of Chignecto Bay from this provincial park.

Five Islands hosts an annual Glooscap Festival in July. A clam festival livens up the nearby community of Economy in August. During the winter, cross-country skiers use park roads and the Economy Mountain Trail to enjoy the blanketed park and the hush that snow brings upon the land.

Directions: From Truro, follow Highway 102. Take Exit 15 to Highway 104, then take Exit 11. Follow Route 2 on the Glooscap Trail to Five Islands Provincial Park.

Victoria Park

20

Perhaps urban parks are testimony to a deep-seated need for wilderness and wide open spaces. Even the most devoted urbanite will find pleasure in Truro's Victoria Park. The park is 162 ha (400 acres) of wooded trails, scenic views, and waterfalls situated in the centre of town, an inviting haven for families, fitness buffs, and nature lovers of all ages. Cross-country skiers and orienteering enthusiasts are drawn here, too.

Victoria Park is a natural haven in the midst of urban life.

Generations of visitors have the community-minded Ross and Waddell families to thank. In the late 1800s they generously donated the land for what has evolved into one of the province's finest urban parks. In return, two accessible waterfalls are named in their honour.

Geologists come here to "read the rocks" and uncover the mysteries locked within. Their discoveries tell a fascinating tale of geological action. Victoria Park offers a good example of how running water can sculpt the land. Scientists say the benign-looking Lepper Brook, which zig-zags through the park is re-eroding the ancient Triassic gorge through which it flows. Running water created most of the land forms in the park, but glaciers played a role as well. Lepper Brook valley was etched deeper from glacial erosion.

The long, tapering crack visible in the valley rocks was probably an earthquake's handiwork. The opening was later filled in with sediments carried in brook flood waters. Talus slopes—areas of loose rocks—have been formed from the action of freezing, thawing, wetting and drying, as well as by tree roots.

Features include several areas of old-growth hemlock, a mushroom-rich ravine, slate ledges, and crevices brimming with glistening cliff-dwelling ferns. There is a full complement of bird life typical to this type of Nova Scotia forest habitat. The

P

terrain is gentle and eight interpretive stations provide information along the trail. It is believed the area was once covered by a dense forest of hemlock trees until clearing was done for Truro's first Roman Catholic Glebe House, which has since been demolished.

The Norway spruce in the park were planted years ago as an experiment to see if the species would thrive. They have become some of the finest specimens to be found in the province.

Some believe the separation of the recreation area from the wilderness trails helps to preserve the pristine appearance of the upper park with its waterfalls, rustic paths, and scenic features. Just inside the park entrance off Brunswick Street is the sports and recreation area, with a pool, playground, tennis courts, a ball field, and a cookout pavilion. In the upland area, rustic walking paths circumvent the brook and the ridges of the gorge and lead to the falls. Wooden stairs stretch up both sides of the gorge. With about two hundred steps, the stairway presents a challenge, but it is well-maintained.

Visitors can hike from the main entrance to the impressive Joe Howe falls. Tour the park on foot for the full effect of the 15m (49 ft.) falls. During most summers, Lepper Brook slows to little more than a trickle. The best time to see the waterfalls is in the spring. There is a 1.6 km (1 mi.) jogging trail at the Participark beyond the gorge.

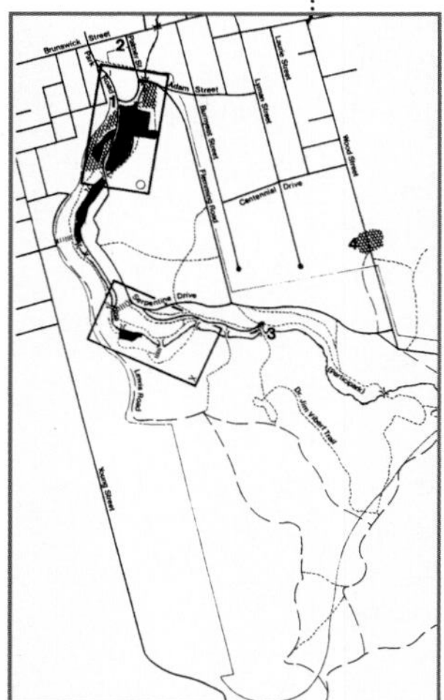

Directions: Victoria Park, open year-round, is located on Park Road, just off Brunswick Street in Truro, which is at the crossroads for the Trans-Canada Highway 104 and Highway 102.

Anthony Provincial Park

This picturesque park provides easy access to the mud flats and beaches of Cobequid Bay. People enjoy exploring the curious habitat of the tidal flats or swimming when the incoming tide is coddled to a comfortable temperature by the sun-warmed expanse of mud. From the public wharf—where mountains of pulpwood were once loaded onto scows and shipped to Hantsport—people of all ages like to tempt a bite from sea bass or flounder. If they're lucky, eagles will show, swooping along the banks of the bay in their own quest for fish.

At this picnic park along the Fundy coast, visitors can make their way to the shore to explore the mudflats and wade at low tide.

This famous tidal bay area is a haven for breeding shorebirds, marsh and upland birds. The colourful pheasant is common in local fields and woodlands. Listen for its harsh squawk. The mud flats are like a sprawling dinner table for migratory bird species such as the semipalmated sandpiper, one of Nova Scotia's smallest shorebirds that feeds on insects and marine organisms, especially a shrimp-like crustacean called *Corophium.*

Route 215, winding past rural communities of the Cobequid Bay, is known for its lovely scenery. Development there is at a minimum. All along this Fundy Shore, the tides are the highest in the world. In 1942, the phenomena drew American scientists to the spot where Anthony Provincial Park is now located.

The local community is developing interpretive displays to highlight historical features of the park and area. For example, the Brown and Anthony shipyard once crafted elegant wooden sailing vessels here. The Historical Society Museum housed in a former Presbyterian church near the park has displays related to the shipbuilding, farming, and fishing industries that once buoyed the local economy.

Directions: From Truro, follow Route 236 to South Maitland. Take the exit to Route 215 toward Maitland. Follow the Glooscap Trail to the Anthony Provincial Park.

Glooscap Trail

22

Burncoat Head Park

Timing is everything at this 1 ha (3 acre) community-run park, where the tide is the main attraction. Two high tides at intervals of twelve hours and twenty-five minutes charge the shore daily. The highest recorded tides in the world—16.5 m (54 ft.)—have been measured in the area of Burncoat Head. The surrounding area is now part of the Tidal Bay Eco-zone of the Fundy Shore.

Ask a tidal specialist about what makes the tides so high and a lengthy explanation may ensue. In addition to astronomical factors, tides are influenced by sizes, boundaries, and depths of ocean basins and inlets. The rotation of the earth, wind, and barometric pressure fluctuations also have some influence.

Burncoat Head, a community-run park, is an excellent spot to see the contrast between high and low tides in the Minas Basin.

Simply put, conditions are just right in the Bay of Fundy area for immense and powerful tides. A map of Nova Scotia will show the unique geographic configuration of land and sea which has played a part in the tidal phenomenon. Summarizing the reasons for the highest tides isn't easy. Fortunately, marvelling at them is.

Visitors have to visit the newly created park twice to observe the phenomenal contrast between high and low tide. The Bay of Fundy and Minas Basin tides rise and fall an average of 13 m (43 ft.) and over 16 m (53 ft.) during feisty spring tides, when the sun, moon, and earth are in alignment to exert a mighty pull on the waters of the world. As billions of tonnes of water pour through a funnel-like opening 10 km (6 mi.) wide between Cape Blomidon and Partridge Island, the tides exert a profound influence on the coastline.

Gardens and tree-identification signs make a visit to the park pleasant and informative.

Directions: From Truro follow Route 236 to South Maitland then exit to Route 215 to Maitland. Follow the Glooscap Trail to Noel, exiting again to Burncoat.

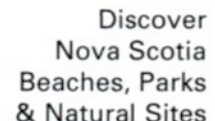

Smiley's Provincial Park

A drive through the region around Smiley's Provincial Park will reveal white gypsum cliffs that are common between Windsor and Brooklyn. Gypsum deposits have produced a topography characterized by round sinkholes, underground streams, and caves

Smiley's is a great place to observe the intriguing Little Brown Bats, *Myotis Lucifugus* (literally, "mouse ears shunning the light"), and their nightly feeding ritual from roughly the end of May to the end of September. The park is nestled in a ravine, protected from wind and other elements. Combined with the presence of the slow-moving Meander River, insects such as mayflies flourish in season.

At Smiley's Provincial Park, a charming swimming hole provides refreshing relief on a hot summer day.

When night falls, grab a flashlight and head toward the bridge, where the Little Brown Bats come for their daily feeding. A second feeding occurs around midnight. If it is raining, bats won't fly, but if a storm is brewing, their frantic activity will be a reliable warning sign.

Unique flora is a highlight of the park. Because the Meander River can flood in spring, a large and fertile floodplain has been created. It is home to a variety of infrequent flora. The entire Meander River intervale has a micro-climate that allows these plants to survive. Naturalists have found a surprising variety of plants within the park, including Indian Pear, large groups of cuckoo flower, toothwort, yellow violets and dog-tooth violets, nodding trillium, red baneberry, wild strawberry, pussytoes, and veronica.

A large playground, horseshoe pits, a wonderful "swimming hole," and a short wooded walking trail are provided. The latter is used year-round.

Directions: From Windsor, follow Route 14 for 16 km (10 mi.) then follow the MacKay Section Road about 0.4 km (0.2 mi.) to Smiley's Provincial Park.

During the summer, lupins line the Sunrise Trail roadsides in thick, colourful clusters.

Sunrise Trail

24 Melmerby Beach Provincial Park
25 Arisaig Provincial Park
26 Pomquet Beach Provincial Park

24

Melmerby Beach Provincial Park

This beach along the Sunrise Trail features the warmest waters north of the Carolinas. Here, visitors have over 80 ha (200 acres) of contrasting landscape to explore consisting of a gently sloping beach, high sand dunes, and washover fans, and the low sandstone coastal formation of Roys Island. The best vantage point for scenic panoramas is from the northern headland peninsula. From the island's southwest limit, the full expanse of the Northumberland Strait, the vertical cliffs of Pictou Island, and the outline of Prince Edward Island are visible.

At Melmerby Beach, on the Northumberland Strait, swimmers delight in the warmest waters around the province.

The long seaward curve of the sandy beach was created by centuries of storm-driven wave action. Melmerby is another example of dune recovery following misuse. Boardwalks and snow fencing are part of an effort to prevent further erosion.

Flora within the park is diverse. A brief farming era led to vegetation varying from weeds and grasses to areas regenerating with white spruce. Common juniper, black crowberry, cinquefoil, dwarf spruce, lichens and hairgrass cling tenaciously to the thin soil of the island's northeast headland.

Some areas of the park are rich with songbirds. Geese and duck are common along the estuary. Some fox and deer find sanctuary here as well. Oyster beds along the Northumberland Strait hold quahogs, dwarf surf clams, and other warm-water molluscs and crustaceans.

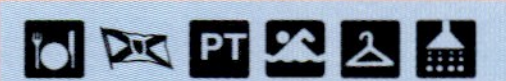

The beach park has salt-rinse showers, full canteen service, and is supervised by the Nova Scotia Lifeguard service.

Directions: From New Glasgow heading east toward Cape Breton, take Exit 24 off Route 104. Turn right at the end of the ramp. Turn right toward Trenton at the second set of lights. At the next Stop sign turn left then follow the signs to Melmerby Beach.

Boardwalks at Melmerby Beach help protect delicate dunes from erosion and make walking at this site enjoyable.

25 Arisaig Provincial Park

While fossils are scarce in southern Nova Scotia, the north is blessed with a bounty. Ordovician and Silurian rocks at Arisaig and in the Cobequid Mountains are rich in fossils, pointing to conditions nurturing to life: warmer water, sunshine, and abundant food. At Arisaig lays one of North

Fossil hunting along Silurian rocks is a highlight at this picnic park.

America's most continuously exposed sections of Silurian age rock. For a century and a half, scientists have made their way Arisaig to document conditions representing the Late Ordovician period (448 million years) through the Silurian period to the Early Devonian period (401 million years).

Visitors are most likely to find impressions of clamlike brachiopods, but cone-shaped nautiloids (predators closely related to modern squid), bryozoans (sea-floor-dwelling moss animals), tentaculites (cone-shaped fossil shells with rings) and crinoids (filter-feeding animals that lived attached to the sea bottom by thin stalks) have all left a record of their existence in the fossil-rich rocks at Arisaig. Interesting fossil finds can be reported to the Nova Scotia Museum. Call (902)424-7357.

Most of what is now the park was farmed by descendants of Highland Scots. They settled large portions of land along the warm waters of the Northumberland Strait in the late 1700s. Fishing and lumbering were defining industries as well. Today, Arisaig Park has a 1.6 km (1 mi.) loop trail which winds toward the shore through a forest of white spruce, starting at an interpretive kiosk that highlights the fossil history and diverse geology. The shoreline portion of the trail includes a viewing platform and beach access spots. Searching for fossils along the beach and near Arisaig Brook is an educational form of treasure hunting. Visitors should use caution near the unstable cliffs. It is recommended to use designated look-offs and to avoid walking under overhanging sections.

The park is officially open from mid-May until mid-October, but holds plenty of appeal for outdoor enthusiasts in the fall, winter, and early spring.

Directions: The park is located on Route 245, west of the community of Arisaig—27 km (17 mi.) north of Antigonish and 57 km (36 mi.) northeast of New Glasgow.

26 Pomquet Beach Provincial Park

The sand dunes at Pomquet Beach are renowned as Nova Scotia's finest example of dune succession. Exceptionally diverse vegetation and fauna are found in the dune system, which forms a wide barrier beach across the harbour and has made Pomquet a site of ecological significance. No other dune system in the province supports the type of forest ecosystem found here, characterized by a mixture of deciduous, coniferous, and mixed wood trees. Wetlands lay between former dune ridges, providing birds and other wildlife with a habitat in which to feed and breed.

Pomquet is growing bigger thanks to geological action. Waves from the open sea reach the side of the sheltered, cup-shaped St. George's Bay at such an oblong angle that the result is what scientists describe as a "strong, longshore movement of sediment." Pomquet serves as an ideal holding vessel: Some 50,000 m^2 (65,000 cu. yards) of sand—or roughly 4,600 dump truck loads—are deposited here by nature each year.

The history of the beach's evolution is explained by interpretive signs along a boardwalk. A primary dune backed by no less than a dozen older dune

Pomquet Beach is one of the best examples of dune succession in the province and supports a unique type of forest ecosystem.

ridges represents about eleven hundred years of development. Scientists believe the relatively small difference in height between the ridges suggests that the system formed fairly recently, possibly in the last thousand years.

Biologist and Pomquet resident Bob Bancroft leads walks at the park which highlight a surprising diversity of natural attractions. One of his first stops is at the top of a drumlin, where visitors get a lovely panoramic view of the area, including

A stroll along Pomquet Beach will inspire a deeper appreciation for the ever-changing shores of Nova Scotia.

Pomquet Island where cormorant colonies nest, and St. George's Bay where blue herons are common in summer. Also in summer, wild roses lend their cheerful pink blush to the landscape. Beachcombing is a rewarding experience year-round.

Foxberries, blueberries, and huckleberries grow in abundance around the beach, and black bear have been known to swim across the estuary to reach them. Eagles nest in the harbour area, feeding on carrion and hunting for eels, gaspereau, sea trout, salmon and mackerel. The huge birds of prey survive on overwintering waterfowl.

The five Acadian families that first set foot at Pomquet in the latter part of the 1700s were greeted by the spectacle of a dune-capped shoreline fringed with deep green forest that still exists today. Pomquet continues to honour its Acadian heritage. In February, the winter festival gets underway; Acadian flags are unfurled, and traditional costumes are donned with pride. Parades, dances, sporting events, Acadian cuisine are all part of the celebration.

In the late 1930s, vast quantities of sand were taken from Pomquet Beach to use in the building of nearby St. Francis Xavier University; the demand for winter road sand was met from the same source. Pomquet is rejuvenating well and is now a protected beach.

Although Pomquet is a deservedly popular beach, visitors should be aware that poison ivy grows in dunes and grassland areas, and jellyfish are found in swimming areas during the summer months. Nonetheless, the beauty and wonder here make exercising a little caution worth the visit.

Directions: From Antigonish drive east on Highway 104 for about ten minutes. Watch for the Pomquet sign. Turn left and head up the hill. Signs clearly mark the way to the provincial park.

Cape Breton Trails

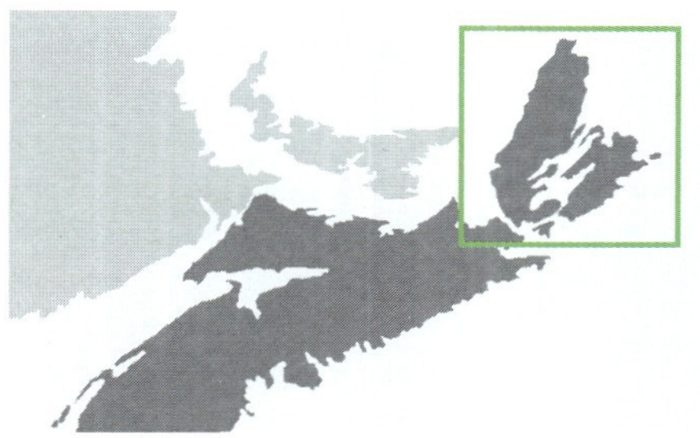

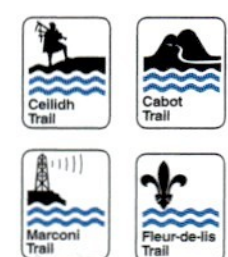

- **Ceilidh Trail**

27 Port Hood Provincial Park
28 Lake Ainslie-Margaree River System
29 Whycocomagh Provincial Park

- **Cabot Trail**

30 Cape Breton Highlands National Park
31 Cape Smokey Provincial Park
32 North River Falls Provincial Park
33 Uisge Ban Falls Provincial Park

- **Fleur-de-lis Trail, Marconi Trail & Metro Cape Breton**

34 Mira River Provincial Park
35 Kennington Cove
36 Dominion Beach Provincial Park

27

Port Hood Provincial Park

The chunks of coal that occasionally surface on the provincially owned beach at Port Hood on the west side of Cape Breton are reminders that mining once sustained such communities. When stone was quarried on Port Hood Island to build the fortress at Louisbourg in the early 1700s, a small coal seam along the mainland shore yielded fuel for heat and light to guide the miners' way. Port Hood Island is just one of over thirty-six hundred islands along the province's extensive coastline.

Port Hood Provincial Park offers swimming and boardwalks. A short boat ride to Port Hood Island—a good bird-watching site—is part of the enjoyable experience at this mainland park.

Through community efforts the beach has become a popular recreation site with boardwalks and basic amenities. The park boasts a fine (unsupervised) swimming spot with sloping shore and comfortable water temperatures.

The village of Port Hood on Route 19 offers shops, services, and a public wharf. Only a kilometre or so offshore, the former fishing community of Port Hood Island is now a welcome haven for the summer home owners when warm weather arrives.

Bertie and Shirley Smith, descendants of one of the first settlers who came from Cape Cod in 1786, are island caretakers off-season. Those who crave a closer look at this marvellous island can charter a boat and spend a day exploring the marine-influenced landscape that is roughly 5 km (3 mi.) long and 2 km (1.5 mi.). Other than a small canteen run by the Smiths, there are no shops, services, public phones or other commercial distractions.

Bird life is abundant on Port Hood Island. Heron, osprey, and nesting bald eagles gather here. Points of interest include the old quarry on the western side, the Jubilee United Church circa 1904, and an old cemetery.

Directions: From the Canso Causeway, take Route 19 to Port Hood, approximately 45 km (28 mi.). To charter a boat to Port Hood Island, to book a bilingual walking tour of the island, or a deep sea fishing excursion call Port Hood Island Boat Tours at (902)787-3490. For ferry transportation call Bertie Smith at (902)787-2515.

Lake Ainslie-Margaree River System

28

The bald eagles that build their huge and sturdy nests along the shores of Lake Ainslie, headwaters of the Southwest Margaree River, have found a sheltered environment rich in food. These birds of prey use their talons to grasp the salmon and gaspereaux for which the region is known.

In 1991, the Margaree—the largest river system in Cape Breton and one of the biggest in the province—became the first in Nova Scotia to be nominated to the Canadian Heritage Rivers System.

The swift Northeast Margaree originates in the Cape Breton Highlands, runs along the Aspy Fault through a steep-sided valley and broadens as a mature stream to Margaree Forks. The Southwest Margaree originates at Lake Ainslie and journeys north to join the Northeast Margaree at Margaree Forks. The combined waters continue north through a wide tidal estuary that leads to the Gulf of St. Lawrence. Lake Ainslie was formed by a ridge of sand, formed after the last Ice Age, which damned the river flowing toward Inverness.

Considered one of the finest salmon rivers in the province, the Margaree welcomes the spring run of grilse (young Atlantic salmon, returning to their native river to spawn for the first time after a winter spent at sea, usually in June. Adult salmon run from June through September and into late fall.

To learn about the natural and cultural history of the region's acclaimed salmon fishery, visit the Margaree Salmon Museum in North East Margaree. Call (902)248-2848 for information. Open from mid-June to mid-October, the facility is dedicated to preserving and interpreting the history of angling on the Margaree. A remarkable collection of vintage rods, reels, and many other fascinating artifacts is on display. Anglers still try to top the record set in 1927 when a 26 kg (57.5 lb.) salmon was hooked at the old bridge pool at Big Intervale.

The Mi'kmaq used the Margaree River for fishing, transportation, and trade. They scoured ochre from the mouth of the Margaree and mixed pigments with fish roe or birds' egg yolk to use for painting.

Provincially rare plants and remnant stands of maple-elm climax forest enhance the valleys. The

The winding Margaree River has several branches. The Southwest Margaree flows from Lake Ainslie.

river system is known for having the greatest proportion of forested floodplain of any river in Nova Scotia.

Fishing enthusiasts enjoy their sport on the Margaree River.

Trout Brook Provincial Park features a picture-perfect beach with unsupervised swimming on the shores of Lake Ainslie. A steep stairway leads to a narrow beach backed by a mixed wooded area teeming with wild roses. White birch, ash, and maple trees shade spots on the beach giving welcome relief on hot, sunny days. The shoreline is shallow, and ideal for young swimmers, and the water temperature is moderate. This is a quiet, uncrowded beach with a soft, white sand bottom. In July, the annual Lake Ainslie Heritage Festival celebrates the natural and cultural history of the area.

Directions: Follow the Ceilidh Trail (Route 19) to Lake Ainslie. The Trout Brook Provincial Park is located 2 km (1.5 mi.) south of East Lake Ainslie on Route 395.

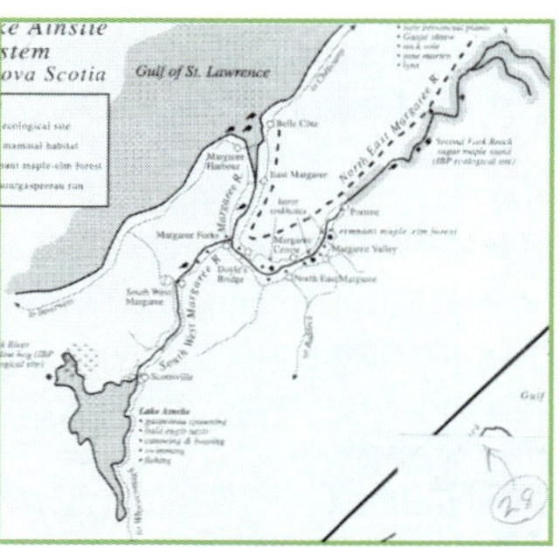

Whycocomagh Provincial Park

An enchanting view characterizes this provincial park. Nestled on a hillside overlooking the Skye River Valley and Bras d'Or Lake, the vista can be enjoyed from the top of the campground or from look-offs along a 2.4 km (1.5 mi.) return hiking trail to the top of Salt Mountain.

The inland Bras d'Or Lake sprawls across 260 km^2 (100 sq. mi.) and with depths that exceed 180 m (590 ft.). The Bras d'Or was created 25 million years ago when submerging land caused flooding in low-lying areas of Cape Breton. The salinity of the lake is half that of the Atlantic Ocean, and the tidal range is very small; so, habitats surrounding the lake are more lush and varied than most ocean coasts.

Whycocomagh Provincial Park has a separate picnic area that overlooks the picturesque Bras d'Or Lake.

Named by aboriginals for its location at the "head of the waters," Whycocomagh first attracted Highland Scots in the early 1800s, who brought their Gaelic song, dance, and foods, among other traditions. Located at the tip of Patrick's Channel, Whycocomagh was once a bustling small port. The village hosts an annual summer festival with canoe races, eagle-watching tours, and ceilidhs.

The park has a boat launch and cooking shelters, and a lovely picnic area at a separate location on the opposite side of Highway 105. Steep stairs lead down to a beach where visitors can revel in the famed Bras d'Or Lake scenery. The campground operates from approximately mid-June to early September. Call (902)756-2448 for further information.

Eagles flourish in this area, and they soar above the lake or perch in trees along the shore. Recently, the eagle population has been used to re-establish a breeding population in Massachusetts.

Directions: The park is located 0.4 km. (0.2 mi.) east of Whycocomagh on Highway 105. Travel 50 km (30 mi.) east of the Canso Causeway on Highway 105 or 110 km (68 mi.) west of Sydney. From Sydney, take the Trans-Canada 104 or 105 heading towards Baddeck. The community of Whycocomagh is roughly 20 km (12 mi.) past Baddeck.

Cape Breton Highlands National Park

This expansive national park in northern Cape Breton is famous for some of the most breathtaking scenery in the world. Much of the spellbinding Cabot Trail traverses the pastoral Cape Breton Highlands National Park. Some say a person needs to travel the roughly circular, 300 km (186 mi.) trail to fully appreciate the real spirit of Cape Breton.

The Cabot Trail winds along the perimeter of the striking Cape Breton Highlands National Park before it turns inland. Dramatic cliffs and seascapes prompt many stops along the way to drink in the spellbinding scenery.

Touted as one of the last remaining tracts of protected wilderness in Nova Scotia, the park is 956 km^2 (366 sq. mi.) of rugged wilderness and sublime coastal scenery.

An ideal wildlife habitat, the national park is one of only four in the world protecting breeding grounds of Atlantic salmon, which is an

internationally threatened species. The fish spawn in most of the park's major rivers. Three-quarters of Nova Scotia's breeding populations of bald eagles are found on Cape Breton Island, including several areas in the park. Although moose (and woodland caribou) disappeared from the island by the late 1800s due to disease and overhunting, descendants of moose introduced into the park in the 1940s may be seen today.

Some consider northern Cape Breton, overlooking the Gulf of St. Lawrence, one of the best land-based vantage points for whale watching from early spring to late fall. Pilot, minke, humpback, and fin whales can be sighted from many coastal sites along the Cabot Trail. Mounted telescopes are supplied at some look-offs from Neil's Harbour to Ingonish to help identify whales frequently found in the area.

Majestic eagles are a common sight in the rugged Cape Breton Highlands.

Aged trees populate deciduous and mixed forests bursting with luxuriant understories of saplings, low shrubs, and ground plants. Rare plants such as yellow mountain Saxifrage and Western Rattlesnake Plantain cling to moist valley slopes. Deep rocky gorges gouge the Cape Breton Highlands and harbour unusual flora. Over one-third of the 210 plant species designated as rare in Nova Scotia are found here.

All these wonders greeted early European explorers who followed John Cabot. He stumbled upon the "new world" in his quest for the Orient,

but historians are divided over where he first touched land. Was it Cape Breton or Newfoundland?

Although the Cabot Trail has been heralded as a magnificent engineering feat that created one of the world's most beautiful drives, those who strike out

Cycling through the Highlands affords a closer look at the shores and sea.

to explore sections on foot may be best rewarded. Trails vary from the wheelchair accessible Bog Trail, where moose tracks or the animals themselves may appear, to such trails as the L'Acadien and the Franey where steep, long climbs lead to breath-taking panoramic views. There are twenty-six designated trails in all, each with unique appeal.

The Visitor's Centre at the Chéticamp approach entrance has detailed information on a wide range of recreational opportunities, amenities, and other services. A nature bookstore is also on site with the

largest selection in Atlantic Canada. There are more than five hundred camping sites; some are non-serviced in backcountry areas. Visitors can swim in salt or fresh water, picnic in a variety of settings, cycle, and fish (a national park licence is required). In the summer of 1997 a $3.5 million upgrade was completed on the Highland Links Golf Course, located in the national park at Ingonish. The Stanley Thompson designed course is popular for its idyllic setting.

A complete list of fees and hours of operation are available by calling 1-800-996-3995 or the park directly at (902)285-2691.

Marine and continental influences result in a varied climate for northern Cape Breton. The northerly location, higher elevation, and the influence of the cold Labrador current and the Gulf of St. Lawrence make weather unpredictable. It's best to come prepared for rain, wind, and fog as well as warm summer days.

Directions: The park covers much of the northern tip of Cape Breton Island between the Gulf of St. Lawrence and the Atlantic Ocean. Enter the park from the Cabot Trail north of Chéticamp or at Ingonish Beach.

Cabot Trail

31

Cape Smokey Provincial Park

Cape Smokey towers 366 m (1,200 ft.) above the Atlantic Ocean. A ghostly mist can linger at the crown of this mountain, a massive block of Late Ordovician pink granite located on the Cabot Trail about 15 km (9 mi.) south of the eastern boundaries of Cape Breton Highlands National Park. However lofty Cape Smokey may appear, it is the lowest of the major mountains along the Cabot Trail.

Moose do meander through Cape Smokey Provincial Park. Evidence of their travels are more likely seen, so step carefully.

The 10 km (6 mi.) return trail that is the highlight of the provincial picnic park entices hikers to explore Cape Smokey with its strategic viewpoints, capturing the grandeur of one of the province's highest peaks. From the pinnacle, the coastal scenery of Cape Breton's eastern seaboard and the Cabot Strait is magnificent. Majestic eagles and a variety of hawks are sometimes seen soaring on the updrafts along the cliff line.

Allow about four hours to hike the trail, which begins through an area of small white birch and wild pin cherry trees, products of post-fire recovery since a 1968 forest fire wreaked damage here. Sheep laurel, wild raisin, and mayflowers are scattered about. The trail winds past yellow birch, spruce, fir, and many plants typical to a thin-till rugged terrain such as blueberries and wood fern.

Hikers can take in the distant scenery that includes, from west to east, St. Ann's Mountain, Kelly's Mountain, and the two small Bird Islands in front of it.

Even in winter, the view from atop Cape Smokey is stunning.

Moose leave tracks and signs of browsing. Those who hike at dawn or dusk may glimpse one of these massive, shy creatures.

Hikers should be aware that cliff lines are constantly eroding and may be unstable. It is recommended people remain behind security fences at all times.

Directions: Cape Smokey Provincial Park is 13 km (8 mi.) south of Ingonish Beach on the Cabot Trail.

P PT

North River Falls Provincial Park

32

Waterfalls give hikers true purpose. Whether the effort involved is big or small, the inevitable sights, sounds, and scents are irresistible. One such scenic treasure, the North River Falls, takes a little doing, but those up for a strenuous 18 km (11 mi.) hike through forests and fields will be rewarded. Allow roughly seven hours return for a hike to this amazing waterfall.

If time or energy does not allow for a lengthy hike, the path down to the river leads to Little Falls in just fifteen minutes in and fifteen out. The path (also used by anglers) begins at the well-maintained picnic facilities at the beginning of the park.

The trail to Big Falls—the highest in the province at 32 m (104 ft.)—is challenging at times and it is best to get acquainted with this slice of nature's finery long after winter is past.

The rugged area was tamed once by a group of stout-hearted families bearing names such as McLean, McLeod, McAskill, and McKenzie. They descended from the Highland Scots who settled much of Victoria County in the early 1800s. It is said that their schoolhouse and tannery once stood near the entrance to the park.

A remnant population of pine marten is found here, and the park includes some of the last available lynx habitat in the province.

The trail offers access to a stunning steep-sided river canyon. Side paths lead to pools often jumping with fat salmon. The North River comes into view twice when footbridges take hikers across. Enjoy the beauty of the falls from the trail or, for those with extra energy, there is a very steep secondary path to a viewpoint high above the falls.

Wildlife like the red fox make the North River Falls Provincial Park home. Visitors can enjoy hiking in a natural setting.

Directions: From Highway 105 take Exit 11 to St. Ann's, continue north to North River. After crossing the bridge, turn left onto the Oregon Road and proceed roughly another 3 km (1.9 mi.) or so to the North River Falls Provincial Park.

P PT

33

Uisge Ban Falls

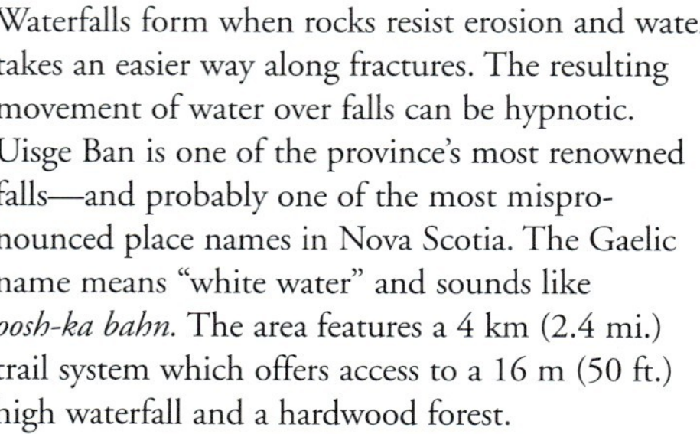

Waterfalls form when rocks resist erosion and water takes an easier way along fractures. The resulting movement of water over falls can be hypnotic. Uisge Ban is one of the province's most renowned falls—and probably one of the most mispronounced place names in Nova Scotia. The Gaelic name means "white water" and sounds like *oosh-ka bahn.* The area features a 4 km (2.4 mi.) trail system which offers access to a 16 m (50 ft.) high waterfall and a hardwood forest.

Owls find ample food supply and mixed forest cover at Uisge Ban Falls. Listen for their distinctive call.

Two well-tended trails lead to Uisge Ban and both are relatively easy for most seasoned hikers. There are some steep spots but they are short. Set aside an hour to make a return hike along the 3 km (1.8 mi.) Falls Trail, which begins with a pass through a field regenerating with white spruce and balsam fir. At Falls Brook the trail heads upstream in a northwesterly direction. A mixed forest habitat gives way to hardwoods and the plants that carpet their roots.

The deep stream valley that leads to the falls is serene with wooden foot bridges, hand rails, and rest stops to assist hikers. Listen for the clamour of the falls as the valley narrows dramatically. Rock voles, weasels, Gaspé shrews, and other small mammals that inhabit the area are rarely seen, but birds such as woodpeckers, warblers, and nuthatches are often visible, or at least heard.

At the end of a long hike at Uisge Ban hikers are rewarded with a spectacular view of the falls pouring down the valley gorge.

The longer River Trail follows along the North Banks Baddeck River, then turns inland, eventually meeting up with the Falls Trail. In autumn, when colours explode from maple, birch, and beech, the sights and sounds that reward hikers when they reach the walls of the gorge which loom on either side of the falls is overwhelming.

A map of the trail is posted in the parking lot.

Directions: The falls are located 14.5 km (9 mi.) north of Baddeck. From Highway 105 take Exit 9 and head toward Forks Baddeck. Turn onto MacPhee's Cross Road; about 1 km (.6 mi.) farther turn left at the intersection and proceed to the parking area.

Mira River Provincial Park

34

The Mi'kmaq traversed the wide and slow-moving Mira River which ambles along southeastern Cape Breton for 40 km (25 mi.) through forests of balsam fir, red maple, white and yellow birch, and sugar maple. The Mira is nestled along a narrow valley that arches from Framboise Cove to Mira Bay.

French settlers saw a grand opportunity in the dense, pliable clay that lined the banks of the Mira River to build a brickyard in the late 1720s and provide building materials for such projects as the Fortress of Louisbourg.

Much of Mira's character comes from the surrounding land: peninsulas, islands, and sheltered coves sculpted by glacial action, which also created a smattering of small lakes at the southern end. Boating and fishing enthusiasts consider the Mira an idyllic destination with its supply of salmon, smelt, trout, whitefish, and gaspereau.

The Mira River has a rich supply of fish and the surrounding bird life is abundant, making the area a popular spot among nature lovers.

Birders value the Mira River Provincial Park with its forests of hardwood and second-growth. Excursions may be rewarded with sightings of bald eagle and osprey, both of which nest along here. Large numbers of the energetic double-crested cormorant fish in the river. In *Birding in Atlantic Canada: Nova Scotia,* Roger Burrows suggests this park as a place to see some of the rarer nesting species, especially in late spring. In late summer, masses of tree swallow fly a quick-winged ballet over the glistening water.

Wild blueberries grow along the banks of the idyllic Mira River.

South, between Forchu Bay and Framboise Cove, are staging areas for migratory waterfowl and shorebirds.

The park has a campground with facilities for the disabled and a boat launch. The day-use beach has unsupervised swimming.

South on the Mira, Two Rivers Wildlife Park features a variety of native Nova Scotia animals along with recreational opportunities.

Directions: The Mira River Provincial Park is located on Brickyard Road, 3 km (2 mi.) east off Route 22 from Albert Bridge; 22 km (14 mi.) southeast of Sydney and 17 km. (11 mi.) from the Fortress Louisbourg National Historic Site.

35

Kennington Cove

The storm-etched shoreline of Kennington Cove was once the stage for two massive military manoeuvres that led twice to the fall of the Fortress of Louisbourg. A monument overlooking the now peaceful landscape tells the story.

Established by the French in 1713, the fortress evolved into an economic rival and a perceived threat to the British colonies. Louisbourg became famous as a military stronghold, a thriving seaport, and a bustling town encompassed in a protected domain. Eventually, a contingent of New Englanders with British naval support attacked and won the fortress in 1745. Handed back to France, the fortress fell a second time into British hands in 1758, and then it was demolished.

Kennington Cove, near the Fortress of Louisbourg, features some lovely flora and is well known for its bogs and fens.

During the 1960s, Parks Canada embarked on a reconstruction project—said to be the biggest in North America—that spanned twenty-two years and cost roughly $26 million. This "living history" site animates eighteenth-century fortress life of Louisbourg and is one of Canada's premier historic parks.

Signs posted along the beach at Kennington Cove warn of rip currents when wave heights exceed 1 m (3 ft.). Roped-off swimming areas are supervised daily from 10 A.M.–6 P.M. in July and August.

The flora in Kennington Cove is unique. The tall herb Angelica that grows around Louisbourg is believed to have come from France. Around the cove, a rare Arctic-alpine species of blueberry, *Vaccinium boreale,* attracts botanists. The cove is also known for its raised bogs (unusual in Cape Breton), and its fens, which harbour rare sedges, the tiny, elusive curly grass fern, and some orchids.

Directions: From Sydney take Route 22 south to the village of Louisbourg. Turn right at the park administration sign. The road to the cove, about 12 km (8 mi.) away, is mainly unpaved. Continue to another park sign, turn left. Follow signs to the cove.

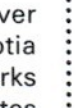

Dominion Beach Provincial Park

Dominion Beach is one of a number of beaches around the province recovering from overuse. The dunes, which once towered as high as 10 m (32 ft.), were washed or blown away or removed by sand mining. In recent years, large rocks were placed on the seaward side of the beach to resist erosion and encourage sand accumulation on the beach front.

The barrier beach of fine white sand at Dominion Beach separates the ocean from Lingan Bay, known as a birder's paradise. Horned lark, piping plover, great blue heron, Savannah sparrow, and greater yellowleg are some species that can be spotted around the area.

An extensive boardwalk helps protect the fragile dunes and connects to the Dominion Heritage Building, an original one-room schoolhouse built circa 1888. Artifacts are on display. On site year-round is a sliding-roof observatory for stargazing. An outdoor interpretive display highlights surrounding bird life and the region's coal mining heritage.

A boardwalk helps protect the delicate dunes at Dominion Beach Provincial Park, where white sandy shore stretches for a mile.

Directions: The park is 8 km (5 mi.) east of Sydney between New Waterford and Dominion-Glace Bay. From Sydney take Highway 4 and from New Waterford follow Highway 28.

The rugged Cape Breton coastline is one of the many natural attractions to this island steeped in Celtic tradition and cultures.

Marine Drive

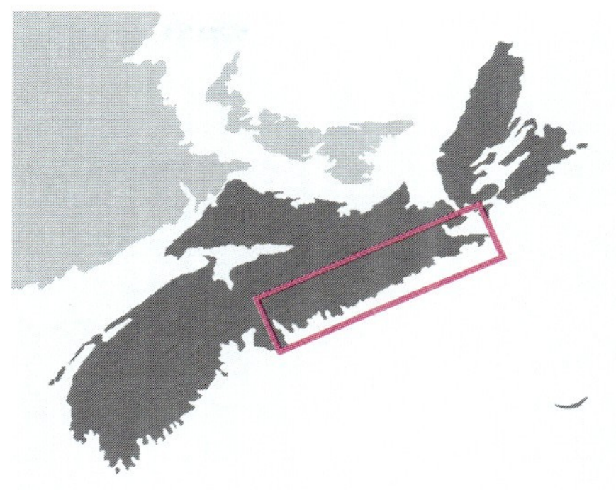

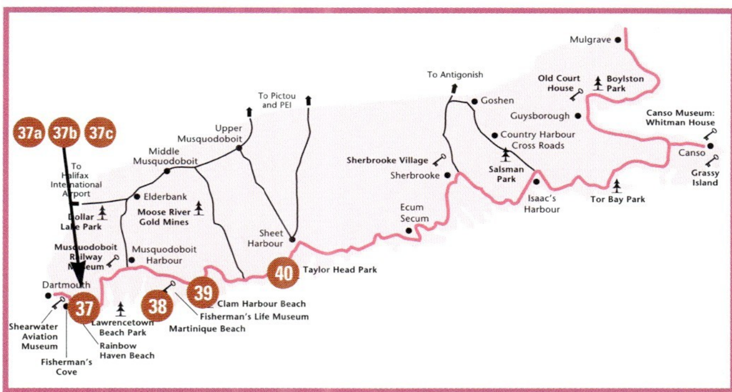

37 Cole Harbour-Lawrencetown Coastal Heritage Provincial Park System

37a Rainbow Haven Beach

37b Conrad Beach

37c Lawrencetown Beach Provincial Park

38 Martinique Beach Provincial Park

39 Clam Harbour Beach Provincial Park

40 Taylor Head Provincial Park

37 Cole Harbour/Lawrencetown Coastal Heritage Provincial Park System

On the fringes of the Cole Harbour business district, a stretch of salt-marsh separated from the ocean by sand dunes and beaches creates a welcome relief from the traffic and din of human activity. Driving east on Route 207 brings coastline scenery into view and opportunities arise for hiking, swimming, and nature walks. Public buses drop off city residents on the doorstep of this unique environmental area. On the other hand, close proximity to the rapidly expanding Halifax/Dartmouth Metropolitan area has put the region from Cole Harbour to Lawrencetown at risk.

The creation of the Cole Harbour/ Lawrencetown Coastal Heritage Park System by the provincial Department of Natural Resources was met with optimism. The large, shallow, saltwater inlet along which Cole Harbour is located is a nurturing ground for many species of flora and fauna. In early spring and late fall large migrating flocks of Canada geese lend special excitement to the area. As many as four thousand have been known to set down here before continuing their migration. Early settlers relied on geese and ducks as an important food source.

Diverse habitats along this park system allow for excellent bird watching opportunities.

Birding enthusiasts enjoy this area year-round as a marvellous place to count species and look for rarities. The area between Dartmouth and Chezzetcook combines almost every kind of habitat found in the province. Woodland birds, shorebirds,

and waterfowl are found in quantity. For instance, the mouth of nearby Musquodoboit Harbour has the largest wintering flocks of Canada geese and black ducks in the Atlantic Provinces.

One needn't be a bird watcher, however, to enjoy all this area has to offer. For further information on cultural and natural history, visit the Cole Harbour Heritage Farm Museum and Tea Room at 471 Poplar Drive or call (902)462-0154.

Various sites within the Cole Harbour/ Lawrencetown Coastal Heritage Provincial Park follow from 37a to 39a.

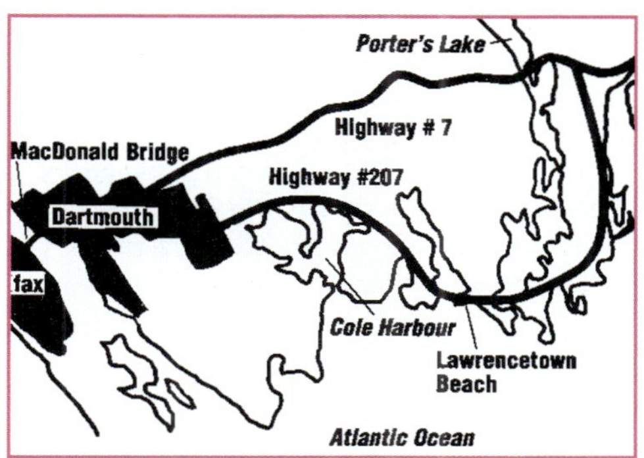

37a

Rainbow Haven Beach

A left turn at Bissett Road and a kilometre farther, near a large old barn on the left is the spot where the first good view of the Cole Harbour saltwater inlet can be seen. This is also the start of the proposed day-use park area, encompassing roughly 242 ha (600 acres). Visitors may park by the barn and explore the hiking trail (popular with birders) that consists of a series of loops through fields and woodlands, and leads down to the shore.

Swimming at Rainbow Haven Beach is a popular summertime activity for the whole family.

Continue to the end of Bissett Road, turn left; the sign for Rainbow Haven Beach Provincial Park comes into view almost immediately.

On a summer weekend, the parking lot at Rainbow Haven may overflow, and the beach is alive with swimsuit-clad visitors. Visitors will find all the convenient amenities.

One local naturalist says the site has improved “100 per cent” since about 1984, when the province created the park. Rainbow Haven has enjoyed dramatic rehabilitation. Boardwalks allow access to the outer beach without tramping over delicate dunes and plant life.

Nature lovers will enjoy watching Nova Scotia’s largest shorebird, the whimbrel, and the Hudsonian godwit rummage in the nutrient-packed salt-marsh. Peak migration for legions of waterfowl and shorebirds takes place between August and September. Great blue herons cleverly flush fish from ribbons of eel grass and spartina. At low tide, Canada geese feed on the roots of exposed plants. Black ducks nest around the harbour and can be seen close to shore all summer, often with broods of ducklings in tow.

Sandy shores at Rainbow Haven are perfect for beach play.

Leaving the park, the road loops past the Dartmouth Trap and Skeet Club—the oldest in Eastern Canada.

Directions: From Dartmouth, head east on Portland Street (also known as Cole Harbour Road and Route 207). Turn right onto Bissett Road toward Rainbow Haven Beach, the first public site along the park system.

Conrad Beach

37b

Those who know of the history of this beloved beach area and its treasures treat this designated International Biological Site with reverence. A haven for rarer birds, the surrounding marshlands teem with life. Shorebirds are fun to watch, plunging their beaks into the mud for food. On a stroll along the boardwalk that leads to the beach, birds soar above the marsh grass. The willet is a vocal shorebird, daring enough to fly close overhead. Red-winged blackbird and sharp-tailed sparrow add their own music to the cacophony. Piping plover struggle to nest in this delicate terrain, home as well to the rare, low-to-the-ground Cotula plant. Usually the traipsing of foxes, bear, deer, and other mammals in the area is not witnessed by visitors, but signs of them may be seen.

A path above Conrad Beach leads to Fox Point, where abandoned, weather-worn fishing shacks testify to the changing times.

Visitors can head straight to the beach for adventure and exploration. At low tide, a hike along the grassy path above the beach to Fox Point leads to the ruins of a storm-battered wharf and fishing shacks.

This is a beautiful beach to walk on; however, the area is not suitable for swimming due to dangerous undercurrents. For those eager to swim, lifeguards are posted at the nearby beaches of Rainbow Haven and Lawrencetown.

The path that leads left from the boardwalk at the piping plover sign circles around a sand and grass path in a large loop to the beach and features one of the province's best examples of dune succession. Seaward, the younger dunes rely on marram grass, orach, sandwort, and sea rocket for stabilization. Inland, the oldest dunes are now crowned with sizeable spruce.

Directions: From Rainbow Haven Beach, return to Route 207 and continue east toward Conrad Beach. Watch for a scenic viewing spot at the crest of Long Hill. Turn right at Conrad's Road and drive to the small gravel parking area at the end of the road.

37c Lawrencetown Beach Provincial Park

Lawrencetown Beach is touted as Nova Scotia's surfing beach, but the best conditions are found from late November to the end of April. According to author, resident, and surfing aficionado Lesley Choyce, those who lug their boards to the beach in the summer may be disappointed.

The park has a large modern beach centre and lifeguard services. Nonetheless, swimmers are advised to stay in designated areas; powerful currents make swimming in surrounding waters dangerous. There are warning signs posted on Route 207.

For a memorable view of the surrounding area, climb the hill to the MacDonald House Tea Room and savour the scenery over hot tea.

For avid surfers, "surf's up" at Lawrencetown Beach from late November to the end of April, when waves are prime. Panoramic ocean views are enjoyed here.

Visitors to Lawrencetown Beach can expect to see (or use their own) brightly coloured wind sails on the waves.

Directions: From Conrad Beach, Lawrencetown Beach is located further east. Return to Route 207 and follow road signs for Lawrencetown Beach.

Martinique Beach Provincial Park

A sparkling crescent of fine, white sand joins Flying Point Island to the mainland. Open and wooded picnic areas, boardwalks, and walking trails along a beautiful coastal landscape make this a great destination.

A single primary dune ridge runs the length of the beach system. To the west, large clumps of beach pea mingle with spicy yarrow in the sandy till. Seaside goldenrod, pearly everlasting, and evening primrose grow over the crest and back slope of the dunes. At the western end lies a typical dune heath of crowberry, ground juniper, cranberry, myrtle, and reindeer lichens. Blown sand takes its toll on the flora; the area is gradually reverting to beach grass.

Ponds, flats, and shallow areas throughout the lagoon support eel grass flats. Fish, waterfowl, and invertebrates seek shelter in these beds.

Fall can be a lovely time of year for a beach walk at Martinique.

Behind the beach lies a large lagoon at the head of Musquodoboit Harbour, a provincial game sanctuary and perennial gathering grounds of the Canada goose—the largest overwintering flock in Eastern Canada. The lagoon is one of the most productive areas for shorebirds and waterfowl on the province's Atlantic coast.

Deer inhabit the provincial game sanctuary located behind the beach park.

Heron and osprey frequent Martinique Beach. In early April and October, the site is an important stopover for Nova Scotia's Ipswich sparrow, which nests almost exclusively on Sable Island. Piping plover and semipalmated plover, spotted sandpiper and willet breed on the beach, so step with care in spring and summer.

Directions: From Dartmouth, take Route 107 toward Porters Lake and Musquodoboit. Turn right onto Route 7. Turn right at Petpeswick Road and watch for Martinique Beach signs.

Clam Harbour Beach Provincial Park

A beautiful white sand beach combined with creative imaginations are the makings of the annual Clam Harbour Beach Sand-Sculpturing Contest. At the end of the day, judges bear the tough task of choosing the winners based on originality, design, and detail. The mid-August event attracts throngs of people to this spot each summer. This provincial park beach is a popular spot, too, for sunbathers, beachcombers, swimmers, and picnickers who are drawn to the stretch of hard white sand and sun-warmed shallow waters.

Undeveloped trails lead to many quiet scenic spots along the beach and salt-marsh. In summer, the trails are brightened by wild roses, blue flags (wild iris), violets, and beach peas. The cranberry marsh behind the beach is enticing in fall when the berries are ripe for picking.

Centred on a peninsula in Clam Bay, the park is the main ocean beach of Nova Scotia's Eastern Shore Seaside Park System, extending eastward from Lake Charlotte to Taylor Head.

The area has a typically deeply indented coastline with rugged, exposed headlands protruding into the Atlantic and covered with coastal forest of black spruce, fir, and birch. At the turn of the century, sailboats navigated around Burnt Island. Shoreline erosion quickly changed the topography as waves wore away at exposed drumlin deposits. As recently as forty years ago, Burnt Island was separated from the mainland by water.

Clam Harbour beach hosts the annual Clam Harbour Beach Sand-Sculpting Contest, which draws scores of skilled and artistic sculptors in August.

Today the combination of pristine wilderness areas and a close proximity to urban centres, such as Dartmouth, enhance the growing recreational opportunities for outdoor enthusiasts.

Amenities include a canteen, an interpretive display, and supervised swimming. A series of ramped boardwalks offer accessibility by connecting the main parking lot, beach centre, and beach area.

Directions: The park is located 84 km (51 mi.) east of Dartmouth on Route 7. At Lake Charlotte, turn right and proceed to the park.

Marine Drive

40

Taylor Head Provincial Park

Roughly a thousand million years ago, the area that is now Taylor Head Provincial Park sat in the centre of a supercontinent. When the land mass divided, new oceans formed along the rifts. Over millions of years later, several kilometres of sand, silt, and clay eventually formed the rocks at Taylor Head. Taylor Head is one of only a few places in the province where "sand volcanoes" are found.

Park boundaries encompass habitats as varied as the waterfowl and seabirds which breed in abundance on offshore islands, including Arctic tern and common tern, black guillemot, Leach's storm petrel, and common eider. Canada geese and black duck migrate through the park in spring and fall.

Taylor Head Provincial Park offers four hiking trails. Scenic coastal views and varied habitat from barrier beach to spruce-fir forest are part of their appeal.

Four park trails provide access to the varied habitats and scenic vistas. The Spry Bay Trail loops past coastal barrens and forests of spruce and fir, boulder-strewn shores, coastal fresh marsh, and an inland barren. Expect about three hours of hiking to explore this 4 km (2.5 mi.) trail.

The 3 km (2 mi.) Bob Bluff Trail follows the edge of the Pyches Cove coastline, passes through a coastal barren and a spruce and fir forest, and overlooks the islands of Mushaboom Harbour. The sandy shore of Pyches Cove Beach is ideal for those who enjoy bird watching.

Bull Beach Trail, about 6 km (3.5 mi.) of coastal scenery, leads to a spruce and fir forest overlooking Mushaboom Harbour. Seaward sand dunes support American beach grass and sea rocket. Bayberry, cranberry, foxberry, and white spruce cling to older dunes further inland.

Interpretive displays highlight the trails. The bogs found scattered throughout Taylor Head teem with botanical treasures such as Bake-apple and starflower.

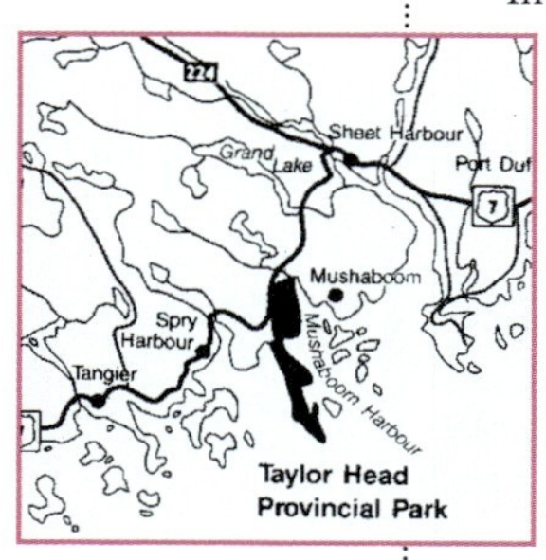

The park is officially closed by mid-October, but some outdoor enthusiasts prefer the solitude of an off-season trek.

Directions: The park is located 0.4 km (0.2 mi.) east of Spry Bay and 11 km (7 mi.) southwest of Sheet Harbour on Route 7.

Halifax Metro Area

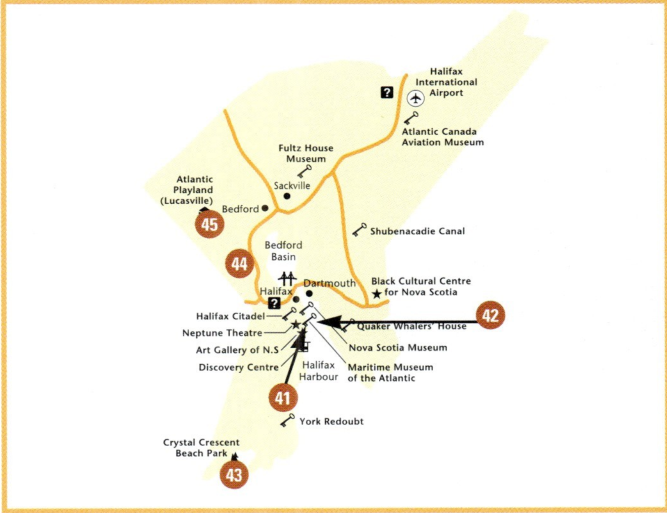

41 Point Pleasant Park
42 McNab's Island
43 Crystal Crescent Beach Provincial Park
44 Hemlock Ravine
45 Lewis Lake Provincial Park

41 Point Pleasant Park

Located on the southern tip of the Halifax peninsula, near the downtown core, Point Pleasant Park is a woodland oasis with coastal views that offer respite for city residents weary of urban life. Walkers, runners, cyclists, and cross-country skiers turn out in droves on agreeable days year-round to revel in the serene outdoors.

Point Pleasant Park is a nature getaway situated in the heart of Halifax's South End.

From a geological perspective, the park area was formed about 500 million years ago, when vast quantities of deep sea mud were deposited here. The resulting bedrock of slate was crushed and folded during tumultuous mountain building. Molten masses of granite pushed their way onto the landscape before glaciers gouged and moulded the terrain.

Walking trails 39 km (24 mi.) in total length wind through woods and along shoreline, traversing the same ground as soldiers when the area served as an important British military outpost. An elaborate defence system built in the 1700s that guarded against French troops has mostly deteriorated into moss-covered ruins.

A guide to walkways and points of interest is located at the western entrance on Tower Road. Visitors can explore places such as Point Pleasant Battery with its "high energy" beach, named so for the aggressive waves and swells that batter the land and cart sand away. Quarry Pond, a former slate quarry turned pastoral spot, is worth a visit for the water-lilies and inviting tree-shaded benches.

On the southern tip of the park, a memorial honours navy and merchant sailors. In this vicinity, a ballast heap removed from docking vessels was once kept. European plants that eventually naturalized, such as celandine—once a source for yellow dye—can be found in the area.

Delicate Scotch heather that forms a thick carpet of mauve and green along Heather Road and

near the Sailor's Memorial is a poignant reminder of the area's military past. Some people believe the non-native plant was brought here by British soldiers, who used it as mattress ticking.

In the fall, the leaves of copper beech that line trails in the centre of the park turn brilliant colours. These, too, were brought from Europe. Just beyond Black Rock Beach, several Douglas fir, transplanted from the west coast of North America, tower along the eastern trail facing the harbour.

While military history is crucial to the park's identity, most visitors appreciate the park as a 75 ha (186 acre) sanctuary for wildlife and an outdoor haven for recreation.

Annual events take place at Point Pleasant Park. During the Polar Dip people test their endurance against winter's chill.

Urban forests such as Point Pleasant Park also play an important role in helping to reduce pollution and conserve energy. One shilling—the annual rental fee set by Queen Victoria in 1866 for 999 years—is a small price, indeed for such a valuable park.

Directions: Follow South Park Street or Tower Road in Halifax; these are the park's most popular access points.

42

McNab's Island

The lively birdsong that welcomes visitors to McNab's Island says a lot about this special place. Abundant bird life is, after all, one of the best indications that habitats are healthy and thriving. More than two hundred bird species have been identified on or around the island. Great blue heron, bald eagles, and osprey all nest on this 400 ha (1,000

McNab's Island sits in the mouth of Halifax Harbour.

acre) island on the eastern side of the mouth of Halifax Harbour. A recent bird list noted two "small and secretive species": a pair of saw-whet owls and a sora rail "singing in cattails near McNab Pond."

The Friends of McNab's Island Society filled a book—*Discover McNab's Island*—of facts and lore on surprisingly diverse natural, cultural, and military history. The publication includes information on the adjacent Lawlor and Devils Islands. The Society has also developed an information brochure which includes a map and points of interest, from Hangman Beach—a gruesome reminder of the decade or so around 1800 when deserters were brutally killed and their bodies left to hang as a warning to incoming sailors—to the Findlay's Amusement Grounds, a favourite family spot at the turn of the century. This is where Nova Scotia's renowned carnival king Bill Lynch got his feet wet working rides and concession stands.

Evidence that people have long been drawn to the resources on this small island was found in the

form of aboriginal shell middens (refuse piles) roughly sixteen hundred years old. Flush with wildlife and covered with thick forests, McNab's drew the attention of early European settlers who fished, farmed, hunted, and logged. Except for a smidgen privately held, McNab's is currently owned as parkland by provincial and federal governments.

The island's strategic location in the mouth of Halifax Harbour made it an appealing location for military purposes. The island has had four major forts and a rifle range built on it over the years. Fort McNab National Historic Site, on the south end, and Fort Ives, on the northwest tip of the island, are open to the public. Built between 1888 and 1892, Fort McNab was the first battery to mount breechloading guns, which made it more powerful than others around the harbour at the time.

A century ago, nearby city residents boarded boats and headed for McNab's Island whenever the chance arose for picnics, recreation, and social events. For many years—roughly 1870 to 1930—McNab's was the place to go on Sunday; families travelled on the *Halifax-Dartmouth* to cross the harbour. Frederick Perrin created a Victorian estate here and imported hundreds of plant species to liven up the landscape.

In recent years, McNab's has attracted biologists, naturalists, students, teachers, and nature lovers. Today, visitors enjoy berry-picking, bird watching, cycling, and beachcombing. Those who can secure the services of a charter boat in winter can indulge in ice skating on McNab Pond, cross-country skiing, and snowshoeing. There is no drinkable water or food facilities.

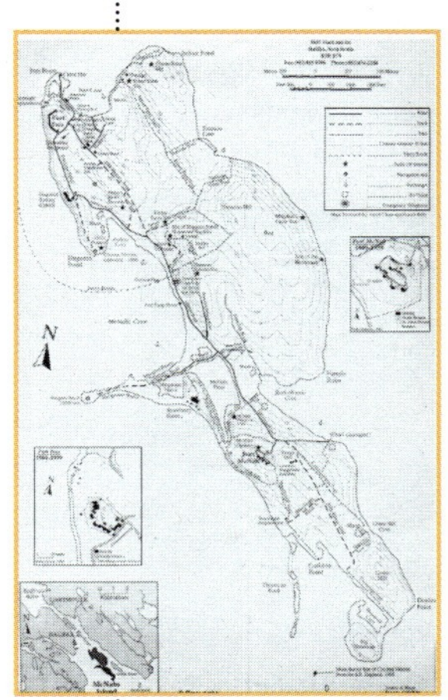

Directions: Either a thirty-minute boat ride, seasonally, from downtown Halifax, or a four-minute ferry ride from Eastern Passage via the McNab's Island Ferry that travels year-round carries visitors to the shores of this wilderness island. Lawlor and Devils Islands are accessible only to those who arrive by small boat. For further information about the McNab's Island Ferry call 1-800-326-4563.

43

Crystal Crescent Beach

Despite the winding road, the route along the Halifax shoreline is well-travelled in summer as city dwellers migrate to the cool oasis of Crystal Crescent. The journey to the beach presents a study in contrasts as rustic fishing villages, colourful yachts, weather-worn wharves and clusters of houses appear along the way.

The sandy beaches at Crystal Crescent are separated by rock outcrops but linked above by a short sand and grass path. Chilly water temperatures keep most people on the beach, but when the thermometer soars, some can't resist a frolic in the refreshing waves.

Crystal Crescent Beach, a short drive from downtown Halifax, is a natural oasis with fresh salt breezes and pounding surf.

There are undeveloped hiking trails at Crystal Crescent, which offer access to a marine habitat typical to the rocky headlands and barrens. This beautiful white granite rock zone is comparable to Peggy's Cove. However, as of the summer of 1997, services were not available.

According to "A Natural History Map of Nova Scotia," "bedrock (along the region) is dominated by granite which forms headlands and knolls elevated well above the adjacent land." Close to shore white spruce are gnarled and stunted by wind and salt spray. Headlands and islands along the coast are important nesting areas for cormorant, tern, and other seabirds.

In July, marshy tracts are lined with bright yellow water-lilies and clusters of wild iris. Coastal scenery is breathtaking, particularly when a midsummer sunset turns the sky lavender.

Wildflowers thrive in summer in the marine habitat around the beach.

Directions: From Halifax's Armdale Rotary, take Route 253 to Purcell's Cove following the southern shore of the Northwest Arm. Continue to Herring Cove and turn left on Route 349, which follows the Halifax Harbour shoreline to Sambro. At Sambro turn left and follow the signs to the beach.

If a cool wind blows a little strong for swimming, it probably is perfect for wind surfing, a popular sport at beaches around the province.

44

Hemlock Ravine

Each spring, in late April or early May, a bevy of yellow-spotted female salamanders creep out from under stones, logs, and clumps of moss and make their way to the heart-shaped pond that has long been a highlight of the Hemlock Ravine Park off the Bedford Highway. The male salamanders arrived a day or two earlier to prepare the site. When their underwater courtship dance is done, males deposit a small cluster of sperm near the female, who then clutches it to her abdomen until egg-laying time. She fixes fist-sized masses of jelly to vegetation at about mid-depth in the water. The yearly ritual has inspired an annual "Salamander Meander" hosted by the Nova Scotia Museum of Natural History, which features a guided night-time visit to watch this intriguing phenomena. While common in Nova Scotia woods, the amphibians are seldom seen.

Along serene woodland trails at Hemlock Ravine the only sounds may be chattering squirrels and bird song.

Of course, the pond wasn't built to accommodate salamanders' breeding habits. Prince Edward, Duke of Kent, who had come to Halifax as commander-in-chief of British forces in Nova Scotia, had his mistress in mind when he set about refurbishing the grounds of a 200 ha (500 acre) rustic estate, which he borrowed from his friend Lieutenant-Governor John Wentworth.

Inspired by his love for the fetching Julie de St. Laurent, the Duke of Kent created an elegant country estate with meticulously landscaped grounds, an Italianate two-storey lodge, stables, formal gardens, coach-houses, and many other enhancements suitable to royalty. Historians say the estate reflected

P

the landscaping trends and tastes of the times. Festive soirées and gala concerts were held in the music room rotunda, with its ceiling resembling a "night sky" painted blue with white stars.

The pond and the domed rotunda—neither of which are in their original state—are all that remain of Prince's Lodge, the name by which it was known at the time. Contrary to popular belief, the original pond was made heart-shaped long after the Duke died. The forest has laid claim to the ruins of other buildings built by the prince.

Towering trees are one trademark of the ravine that includes hemlocks more than three centuries old.

Growing interest in the romantic history of the former pleasure garden, along with a desire to protect the old-growth hemlock forest and other natural highlights, led to the creation of the 81 ha (200 acre) public city park.

Now filled with brown ducks and lily pads, the pond marks the beginning of the named walking trails that wind throughout the park. A large interpretive map at the park entrance gives visitors an overview of this unique ecological site, where Lady's-slippers, Indian-pipe, clintonia, rhodora, twinflower, lambkill, painted trillium, lichen, and fern share the landscape with towering hemlocks, some of which have endured for over three and a half centuries.

Traffic sounds from the usually busy Bedford Highway fade as visitors are enclosed by the tranquillity of the tree-studded ravine, home to ruffed grouse, Little Brown Bats, flying squirrels, white-tailed deer, among other wildlife species.

In summer, the cool canopy is especially inviting to walkers, joggers, and the occasional mountain biker, although the park is open year-round.

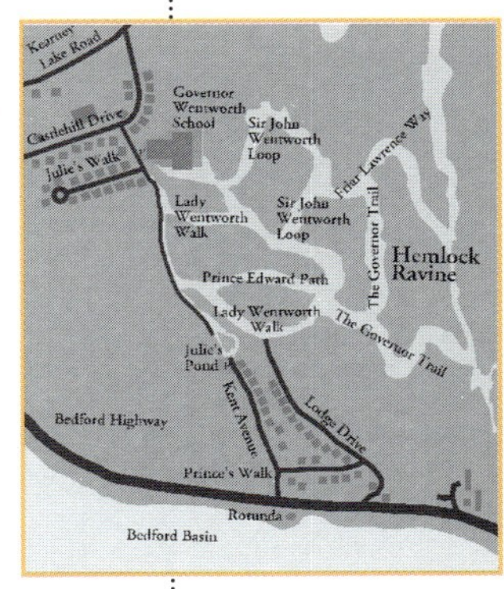

Directions: From Dartmouth, take the Bedford Highway. Turn left onto Kent Avenue opposite the rotunda. Proceed to the top of the hill and watch for a parking lot where the street dips down at the end.

Halifax Dartmouth

Lewis Lake Provincial Park

This award-winning provincial park offers access to a wide range of outdoor recreation activities. Well-marked walkways, wheelchair-accessible nature trails, and scenic viewpoints are found here.

At Lewis Lake Provincial Park, visitors enjoy nature trails, boardwalks, and fishing from the two piers on the lake.

Accessibility makes the park ideal for seniors as well. The site is part of a government initiative to recognize the particular needs of those who are physically challenged by improving access to most provincial parks.

In 1986 Lewis Lake's unique design was recognized with the Facility Excellence Award, bestowed by the Canadian Parks and Recreation Association.

The most popular places to congregate at the park are the two fishing piers, which were designed to be wheelchair-accessible. The lake is stocked throughout the season with brook and rainbow trout and yellow perch. There is good spring fishing at the pier next to the picnic area. The second pier, east of the first, lies at the end of a short trail. Situated at the deepest end of Round Lake, it is known to offer rewarding summer and autumn fishing. Fishers will need a valid Nova Scotia fishing licence.

Directions: Lewis Lake Provincial Park is located on Route 3, 6 km (4 mi.) south and east of Highway 103, Exit 5.

  PT

Lighthouse Route

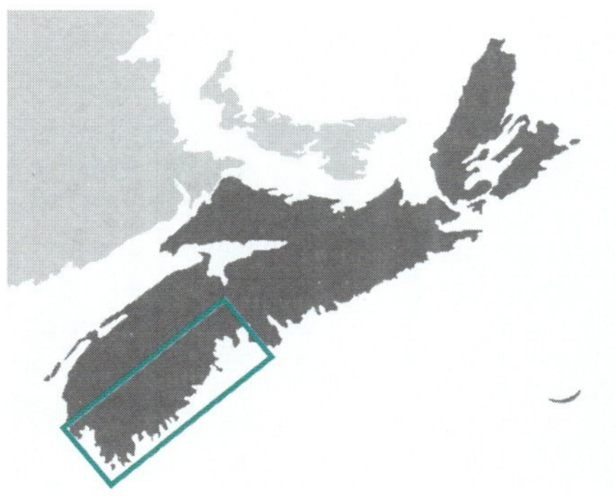

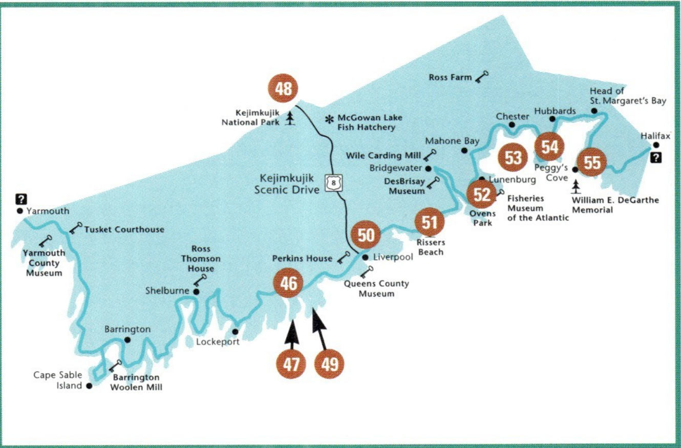

46 Port L'Hebert Pocket Wilderness
47 Thomas Raddall Provincial Park
48 Kejimkujik National Park
49 Kejimkujik Seaside Adjunct
50 Pine Grove Community Park
51 Risser's Beach
52 Ovens Natural Park
53 Graves Island Provincial Park
54 Bayswater Beach Provincial Park / Queensland Beach Provincial Park
55 Peggy's Cove

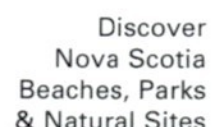

46 Port L'Hebert Pocket Wilderness

Aboriginals once pitched their *wikhuoms* along the Nova Scotia coastline, choosing sites accessible to fresh water, firewood, escape routes, and high ground. Evidence to support the lifestyle patterns of early native life was discovered around the Port L'Hebert area in the form of shell middens. Excavation of the 2,500-year-old refuse heaps has uncovered arrowheads, stone knives, bone harpoons, sewing needles, and other relics.

The Port L'Hebert Pocket Wilderness still offers access to forest and coastal habitat once valued by native people and later by European explorers and settlers. It is said Samuel de Champlain named the harbour in honour of his apothecary, Louis Hébert. Created and maintained by the Bowater Mersey Paper Company Limited, the picturesque park features 3 km (1.9 mi.) of gravelled trails and wooden boardwalks. Huge granite boulders deposited long ago by glacial activity are scattered throughout the woods.

A park trail winds through thick forest to Port L'Hebert Bay. The variety of habitats, coastal (above) and woodland (below), makes this a popular bird-watching site.

Stretching from Highway 103 to the shores of Port L'Hebert Bay, the trail runs through a forest thick with aspen and birch. These young sprout-growth hardwoods are the result of land burned-over many times. Here, visitors will find typical South Shore coastal terrain, where thin soil and water that is brown and acidic from travelling through boggy areas challenged early farmers.

Follow the park trail to a panoramic view overlooking the harbour. On the coast, waterfowl sanctuaries created by the Canadian Wildlife Service include shoreline along the pocket wilderness. Port L'Hebert Harbour is a well-known wintering ground for migrating Canada geese, and thousands stage here in mid-October. The park is one of Nova Scotia's most popular birding areas.

Directions: From Liverpool, take Highway 103 west for about 40 km (25 mi.). The park is located at the Queens/Shelburne County line.

Thomas Raddall Provincial Park

47

The Thomas Raddall is one of Nova Scotia's newest provincial parks. This beautiful 678 ha (1,675 acre) park , situated on the rugged Goose Hills headland overlooking Port Joli Harbour on the scenic South Shore, officially opened in summer 1997. The park is appropriately named for well-known author, long-time local resident, and three-time recipient of the Governor-General's Award for Literature, Thomas H. Raddall. The writer often wove references of the area into his books.

Projectile points, stone knives, bone harpoons, and sewing needles have been unearthed and studied within park boundaries, pointing to aboriginal settlements dating back five hundred to five thousand years. Europeans set down permanent stakes here circa 1786. Later, an inshore fishery flourished in the port, and fish stores and camps thrived along the shore. Today, visitors can explore miles of shoreline dotted with pocket beaches, dunes, and cobble shore.

The multi-use trail is an ideal way for cyclists and pedestrians to explore the park. This is an important nesting area for piping plover, listed as endangered in Canada and the U. S. Wintering flocks of Canada geese are visible from the park. Thousands may gather along Port Joli from September throughout the winter.

There are three shallow freshwater lakes within the park. Fens are rich with sedge, sweet gale, blue joint grass, and cranberry. The sphagnum-filled Moody's Bog along the park's north end is thick with blueberries that flaunt their fiery foliage in fall.

The park has eight walk-in tenting sites and forty-three vehicle campsites adjacent to Port Joli Harbour, with hot water, an unsupervised beach, and a playground.

Directions: From Liverpool or Shelburne, exit Highway 103 in Port Joli at the East Port L'Hebert turn-off.

Along the multi-use trail in Thomas Raddall park, visitors may come upon striking scenes of bird life.

Kejimkujik National Park

Kejimkujik became a National Park in 1968. The area is treasured by Nova Scotians as a beautiful wilderness oasis with 381 km^2 (147 sq. mi.) of inland lakes and forests. Fourteen hiking trails wind through woodlands and along waterways. Hikers and cyclists will enjoy exploring the flora and fauna. Guided nature talks, walks, and canoe trips are available.

When the Mi'kmaq inhabited the area giant white pines over 35 m (115 ft.) high covered the slopes and lowlands of the region. Today, a few groves of eastern hemlock more than three hundred years old survive within the park. Some are along the 6 km (4 mi.) Hemlocks and Hardwoods Trail. The Mersey Meadow and Mill Falls Trails are wheelchair accessible.

There are nature trails throughout Keji that visitors can explore on their own or with a guide.

There is no lack of recreational opportunities. On the contrary, slide shows, interpretive walks, and guided birding forays are readily available to park visitors. Campers can take in presentations at the amphitheatre at Jeremy's Bay Campground, or walk the Beech Grove Trail while listening to a park audio tape that provides details about surrounding woodlands and wildlife. Those who prefer a more rugged and secluded outdoor experience can canoe across Kejimkujik Lake and spend a night at a wilderness campsite.

Hiking opportunities abound in the scenic woodlands at Keji.

By mid-June, many species of birds have congregated. On a typical, sultry summer day, visitors to Keji may wake to the resonant hammering of the showy pileated woodpecker, named for the red crest, or "pileum," on the top of its head.

Other wildlife abounds. For instance, some of Nova Scotia's small population of rare Blanding's turtles are protected at Keji. Watch for them basking in the sun or swimming in the shallows. In late May and early June fawns may be seen grazing on

roadside grasses. The white-tailed deer population is drastically smaller than a decade ago, largely as a result of unfavourable weather and hungry coyotes, but the graceful mammals are still abundant. They thrive on the lush greenery associated with the hardwood habitat that in turn flourishes on the fertile soils typical of drumlins.

A host of different wildflowers take root in woodlands, along lake shores, and in shallow stillwaters. Each season brings forth new blooms. Under softwoods, Lady's-slippers steal the show with their pink hue and unique shape. This orchid works hard before it blooms: it must store energy for several years before it blossoms. Other forest treasures include Clintonia, with its (poisonous) metallic-blue berries, and teaberry, which tastes and smells like wintergreen.

The national park is enhanced by a sister site—the Kejimkujik Seaside Adjunct, near Port Joli. Esteemed as one of the last untouched tracts of sand on Nova Scotia's South Shore, it features intertidal lagoons, rugged headlands, pristine white sand beaches, and a bounty of wildlife. (See pages 82–83.)

Canoeing in Keji is a good way to experience the serenity and beauty of this expansive park.

Forty-four primitive campsites can be found along backcountry trails and canoe routes at Keji. The park affords opportunities for cycling, canoeing, and fishing. Full services are available from late June to early September, and camping is available year-round. Cross-country skiers enjoy the park trails in winter.

Directions: Kejimkujik National Park is located off Route 8, which runs between Annapolis Royal and on the Evangeline Trail, and Liverpool on the Lighthouse Route. Signs to the park are clearly posted.

49

Kejimkujik Seaside Adjunct

There is a quality to this untamed and unspoiled park that inspires respect for the value of preserving wilderness areas. Here, the instinct is to tread lightly amid the serenity. There are no services and camping is not permitted, but a little preparation (carry in drinking water and a portable stove if cooking is required for a picnic) will enhance an unforgettable experience. Places like the adjunct can teach us that less is more.

The beach at the Adjunct is a prime spot for migrating shorebirds from August to October.

The park is accessible strictly on foot via two hiking trails, both of which are rough and wet, although boardwalks ease the way over especially soggy spots. From Southwest Port Mouton (pronounced "Ma-toon") near Willis Lake, an old gravel road leads to the shore at Black Point. This 8 km (5 mi.) return route takes about ninety minutes. The second trail, from the community of St. Catherine's River, is 3 km (1.9 mi.) return and leads to the shore of St. Catherine's River beach. Trails lead to lagoons, tidal flats, and secluded sandy beaches teeming with bird life.

From August to October is the prime time for sighting various species of migrating shorebirds, such as sandpiper and yellowleg. The endangered piping plover may be found here usually nesting among rocks. Vulnerable to crows, gulls, raccoons, and human activity, these shorebirds are one of only a few species that breed in Nova Scotia's coastal habitat. (Most shorebirds seen here in fall

come from the north.) A significant portion of the province's breeding population nest within the park along St. Catherine's River beach and Little Port Joli Bay. Public access is restricted from St. Catherine's River beach from May to mid- to late August, which is nesting season. Birds that never frequent the inland Kejimkujik National Park can be seen at the Seaside Adjunct from August to October, migrating species pause for a time at saltwater lagoons and along sandy beaches.

Thick patches of spruce and fir contrast with grassy headlands and windswept ocean vistas. Cranberry, bog rosemary, and other heath plants flourish in the many moist, mossy areas along the trails. Damp meadows cradle clusters of the purple-fringed orchid.

These two scenes at Cadden lagoon illustrate the untamed quality of the Adjunct, where wilderness is unblemished.

If hikers walk quietly, they may be rewarded with the sight of a white-tailed deer foraging around clusters of spruce trees scattered about the headlands, or a red fox darting into the undergrowth. Harbour seals bask on coastal protrusions around Black Point and Harbour Rocks. The varied habitats within the park encourage equally diverse flora and fauna.

Directions: This day-use wilderness area is located on Nova Scotia's South Shore about 25 km (15 mi.) southwest of Liverpool off Highway 103, and about 100 km (62 mi.) from the inland Kejimkujik National Park.

Lighthouse Trail

Pine Grove Community Park

Wide gravelled walking trails wind through a forest of towering white pines in this 19 ha (48 acre) picnic park established by paper producer Bowater Mersey along the banks of the Mersey River.

The Pine Grove trail system is short, but park planners have included a remarkable assortment of highlights. As hikers today pass by centuries-old pine trees, young mixed woods, and a marshy pond a surprise awaits: an intriguing collection of plant life, some native and some introduced, including Lady's-slipper, Indian groundnut, inkberry, partridgeberry, and teaberry, along with clusters of wild lilies-of-the-valley.

Ducks Unlimited Canada developed a breeding and nesting area for waterfowl and other species at Pine Grove Community Park.

Community groups, such as the Rhododendron Foundation of Nova Scotia, pooled their energies to create a flower-filled park, combining native flora with introduced species. Rhododendrons, azaleas, magnolias, and other shrubs bear identification tags—a helpful touch considering there are more than one hundred varieties of rhododendrons.

One walking trail is named for Captain Richard Steele, a noted international authority on rhododendrons and azaleas, who donated a variety of significant plants to the park. Thanks to the efforts of Steele and others, including plant scientist Dr. Donald Craig who developed rhododendrons suited to the climate, the luxuriant shrubs have become beloved symbols of summer.

Amid the woodlands, huge rocks and boulders wear jackets of lichens and velvety mosses. Glacial action deposited these haphazardly; geologists have studied them to determine in which direction the ice masses moved.

Ducks Unlimited was instrumental in developing a breeding and nesting area for wood duck, teal, great blue heron, and other species. Owl nesting boxes and an osprey platform were placed to encourage birds.

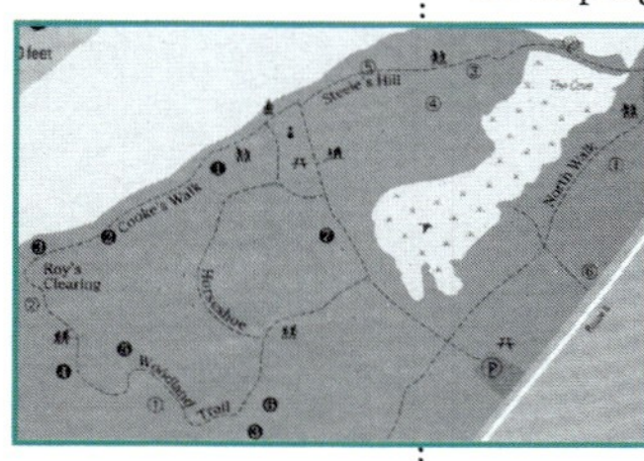

Directions: Pine Grove park is located at the junction of Route 8 and Highway 103 at Milton.

Risser's Beach Provincial Park

51

Risser's Beach boasts just about the warmest water on the South Shore along with predictable surf conditions. Visitors will find a beautiful 1.5 km (1 mi.) supervised beach, a ninety-two site campground with open and wooded sites, and a canteen. The beach is known for its boisterous breakers.

Sand dunes embellish the landscape, playing host to an abundance of pioneering beach plants—sea rocket, American beach grass, sandwort and orach—that stabilize the vulnerable dune system. Further inland, older sand dunes are covered with white pine, white spruce, red oak, and maples. Bayberry, moss, and marram grass abound.

While the sandy beach is the main attraction, visitors enjoy exploring the Salt-marsh Trail via a boardwalk. Salt-marshes are valuable ecosystems, providing food and shelter for migratory waterfowl and shorebirds and raccoon, mink, and muskrat.

Aboriginals reaped riches from the salt-marsh. Sweet grass was favoured for decorative art and traditional ceremony. Some salt-marsh plants, such as glasswort and orach, are edible. European settlers used salt-marsh hay, which was cut and stacked on straddles (platforms) in the marsh.

Look for the somewhat overgrown path behind the interpretive centre. White nuthatches nest along the trail and an unusually dense mat of wild lily-of-the-valley and bunchberry thrives. Just beneath the luxuriant plant covering is a deep bed of sand. Near the end of the trail, a large area with no vegetation supports a vast ant colony.

The varied habitats and beachside camping entice visitors here from mid-May to mid-October.

A boardwalk passes through the scenic marsh.

The sandy beach is the main attraction, but visitors will find wildlife as well at Risser's.

Directions: Risser's Beach is located on Route 331, near Petite Riviere, 14 km (9 mi.) south of Highway 103, Exit 15, or about 26 km (16 mi.) south of Bridgewater.

52

Ovens Natural Park

This privately owned park is as much an experience in sound as it is in sight. Geological formations known as sea caves (renamed "ovens" during the gold mining era) present a unique opportunity for visitors with a taste for natural wonders. Sea caves the size of locomotives were carved by the waves washing through cracks in the slate cliffs. Inside the appropriately named Cannon Cave, for example, there is a resounding *boom!* as waves pound deep in the yawning cavern.

The "ovens" are a series of wave-carved sea caves in slate cliffs that can be explored on foot or by boat. Gold mining was done here from 1862 to 1958.

Sea water gouged gold from the slate and white quartz veins along the cliffs countless centuries before miners moved in and set up primitive ore crushers known as Chilean mills, now on display. Between 1862 and 1958 the district produced over 15 kg (550 oz.) of the precious metal. Gold was found here well before the first official discovery at Mooseland in 1858. The history is explored in a small gold rush museum.

Would-be prospectors are still lured to the area by mainly minuscule bits of gold which constantly erode from cracks and crevices in the cliffs. Geologists say gold frequently occurs as vein or lode deposits in quartz veins in the Meguma Group rocks, originally laid down at the bottom of an ocean as mud and sand. The metal also accumulates as deposits in beach (or river) sediment from the erosion of gold-bearing rocks.

Gold production in Nova Scotia reached its peak in 1898 when almost 900 kg (31,113 oz.) were mined. The Ovens is one of more than sixty "gold districts" in the province, as specified by the Department of Natural Resources.

The park and campground, located on an 81 ha (200 acre) peninsula, ninety minutes southwest of Halifax near the historic town of Lunenburg, offers full services, including a café, housekeeping cottages, and demonstrations in orienteering and gold panning. There is a cliff-top trail, equipped with handrails and viewpoints to admire the "ovens" phenomena. It descends safely into the damp and dripping caves on handy stairways. Guided walking tours and sea cave boat tours are available. The season runs from approximately May 15 to October 1.

Directions: From Lunenburg, travel southwest on Route 332. Turn at Feltzen South Road then onto Ovens Park Road. The drive from Lunenburg takes about ten minutes.

Visitors can safely descend into the phenomenal sea caves via a set of stairs.

53

Graves Island Provincial Park

Graves Island Provincial Park is meticulously maintained and offers swimming, scenic woodland and coastal walking, and picnic tables near a playground.

Remnants of past lives still linger on this island park in Mahone Bay, just a stone's throw from the mainland. Tiger lilies, apple trees, and rose bushes are reminders of those who tended them with care.

Mahone Bay is sprinkled with islands like Graves. As recently as fifteen thousand years ago massive glaciers moulded these elongated or oval-shaped hills known as "humpbacks" for their whalelike silhouette.

Inhabited since the 1700s when German settlers staked their claim, the island was opened as a provincial park in 1971 and now includes roughly 50 ha (123 acres) of fields, white spruce forests, and a smattering of hardwoods surrounded by the sea. Manicured trails wind through woods and along cobble beaches. A man-made sandy beach at the day-use picnic grounds is popular for swimming.

Well-used Trail Number Four skirts a freshwater marsh where a family of muskrats live. Nesting red-winged blackbirds (one of the first birds to return in spring) are at ease in this amphibian paradise, filled with cheerful tree frogs, spring peepers, and leopard frogs. The striking loon forages just offshore and osprey come looking for fish at low tide.

Aromatic sweet gale thrives in this island habitat, along with beach pea, sweet fern (once used to treat poison ivy rash), wild lily-of-the-valley, starflower, and lambkill.

Indian pear, one of the first trees to sprout foliage in the spring, have, in some cases, grown to over 31 cm (12 in.) in diameter—a rarity for Nova Scotia. American mountain ash have also reached unusual size. Some are 10 m (35 ft.) tall and 31 cm (12 in.) in diameter.

Directions: From Chester, take Route 3 east to East Chester. A large sign clearly marks the turnoff to the park.

Bayswater Beach Provincial Park / Queensland Beach Provincial Park

Half the fun in this day-use beach park is the drive it takes to get there. Route 329 hugs the shore of the famed Aspotogan Peninsula, providing opportunities for scenic views of Mahone Bay and the Chester islands.

Bayswater Provincial Beach Park is a delightful rest spot and an ideal place for a leisurely picnic. The roadway divides the park in two: a well-shaded, grassy area with picnic tables beside a freshwater lake, or a sandy beach ideal for a swim or a stroll. There is some boardwalk access, too.

This beach perched near the head of St. Margaret's Bay invites visitors to dam lake water, which runs onto the beach into wading pools for children; to play in the breakers; or build castles that melt away with the tide.

After Bayswater, continue along Route 329 toward Queensland Beach Provincial Park. The road continues along the St. Margaret's Bay shoreline with its rocky inlets and coves strewn with fishing nets, and sailboats gliding out to sea.

Turn right when the road returns to Route 3 and head toward the charming community of Hubbards, beyond which is Queensland. The Queensland Beach sign is posted on a large building called Moore's Landing. Turn a sharp left at the sign and park.

Queensland Beach is perched at the sheltered top of St. Margaret's Bay. Fine, sunny days draw swimmers and sunbathers here. Along the access road are change rooms and pit privies. The surrounding area offers a wide selection of restaurants, inns, and shops.

Directions: From Chester, take Route 3 east. There is an easy-to-spot sign for Bayswater then turn right at Route 329. The park is approximately 20 km (12.5 mi.) from the junction.

Sea kayaking is an increasingly popular activity along Nova Scotia's shores and beaches.

Children frolic in the breakers at Queensland Beach. Fine white sand on the shore can occupy keen sand castle builders for hours.

Lighthouse Trail

Peggy's Cove

Peggy's Cove welcomes well over 100,000 visitors annually. People come from around the world to experience the awesome environment of this quaint fishing village (population about 65). It's no wonder there are ample souvenirs to be had in a smattering of village gift shops. Images of the famous site appear on items from ash trays to T-shirts. The true treasures, however, lay along the wave-battered shore where rock formations and unique flora tell a tale of unimaginable geological upheaval.

Over 470 million years ago, the process began when mud and sand were dumped in a deep ocean basin near ancient Africa. Molten material was eventually thrust upward then cooled and solidified into granite, which was eventually exposed after several kilometres of overlying rock were trimmed off the top by weathering and erosion. Now, granite slabs topped with erratics are testament to eons of geological action. Scoured out depressions have become micro-habitats cradling delicate flora-rich bogs. Plants such as stonecrop, orchids, cotton grasses, and the lovely but carnivorous pitcher-plant delight botanists and tourists alike. Here, adversity encourages survival: delicate little harebells sprout from great chunks of granite in the "spray zone" near the water's edge. Even on fine days, spray and spume are constant companions of the vulnerable village that skirts the cove.

An aerial view of Peggy's Cove.

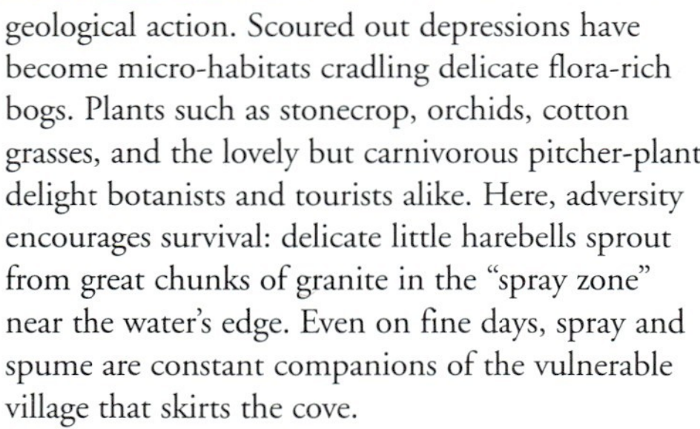

Deep sea divers come ashore at the granite coast of Peggy's Cove.

Settlers who first arrived in the area built boats and set to casting their nets. Peggy's Cove is still home port to inshore fishing vessels. These days, lobster, herring, tuna, pollock, mackerel, salmon, and haddock are hauled in much smaller quantities.

The massive 30 m (100 ft.) sculpted granite monument by the late William E. deGarthe is a compelling tribute to fishermen and their families and is remarkably well-suited to the surrounding landscape.

Picturesque Peggy's Cove lighthouse, rebuilt in

1915, is the only one in Canada to house an operating post office.

Like any seaside village, Peggy's Cove changes quickly when the weather turns. Some people prefer a bright, clear day, while others revel in the atmosphere of a fog-shrouded shore. Whatever the weather, caution is always advised. Large waves often break farther on shore than expected. Shoreline areas and steep slopes should be avoided.

Residents of the tiny community have adapted to an almost continuous influx of tourists. Their neat village homes and gardens, weather-worn fishing shacks, and colorful fishing boats are part of the charm that visitors love to photograph. There are restaurants, accommodations, art galleries, and gift shops to enjoy in the village, along with the natural environment.

Directions: From Halifax, follow Route 333 to Peggy's Cove.

The Peggy's Cove light is a widely recognized symbol of Maritime culture and heritage.

Selected Sources

Atlantic Geoscience Society. "Geological Highway Map of Nova Scotia."

Bishop, Roy, Dr., *The Bay of Fundy's Minas Basin: Highest Tides in the World.* Nova Scotia Marketing Agency.

Burrows, Roger. *Birding in Atlantic Canada. Newfoundland*: Jesperson Press, 1988.

Comfort, Judith. *Rediscover the Lighthouse Route.* Halifax: Nimbus, 1995.

Erskine, Anthony J. *Atlas of Breeding Birds of the Maritime Provinces.* Halifax: Nimbus Publishing/Nova Scotia Museum, 1992.

Derek Davis. *Natural History Map of Nova Scotia.* Halifax: Nova Scotia Museum.

Discover McNab's Island. Halifax: Friends of McNab's Island Society, 1995.

Gibson, Merritt. *Nature Notes for Nova Scotians: Summer, Woodland Animals.* Hantsport: Lancelot Press, 1982.

Griffin, Diane. *Atlantic Wildflowers.* Oxford University Press, 1984.

Hines, Sherman. *Peggy's Cove, Nova Scotia.* Halifax: Nimbus, 1992.

Ingalls, Sharon. "The Duke's Romantic Retreat." *The Beaver Magazine*, June/July 1996.

Institute for Environmental Studies. "Maintenance of Beaches Technical Report." Dalhousie University.

Lacey, Laurie. *Micmac Medicines.* Halifax: Nimbus, 1993.

Lawley, David. *A Nature and Hiking Guide to Cape Breton's Cabot Trail.* Halifax: Nimbus, 1994.

MacLeod, Heather and Barbara MacDonald. *Edible Wild Plants of Nova Scotia.* Halifax: Nova Scotia Museum, 1977.

Murphy, Marty. *A Glimpse of the History of Graves Island.* 1994.

O'Neil, Pat. *Explore Cape Breton.* Halifax: Nimbus, 1994.

Roland, Albert E. *Geological Background and Physiography of Nova Scotia.* Halifax: Nova Scotia Museum, 1982.

Stevens, Clarence. *Birding in Metro Halifax*. Halifax: Nimbus, 1996.

Tufts, Robie W. *Birds of Nova Scotia*. Halifax: Nimbus, Nova Scotia Museum, 1986.

Thurston, Harry. *Tidal Life—A Natural History of the Bay of Fundy*. Ontario: Camden House Publishing, 1990.

The Natural History of Nova Scotia, volumes one and two, Nova Scotia Museum and the Nova Scotia Department of Education and Culture, 1996.

The Blomidon Naturalist Society. *A Natural History of Kings County*. Wolfville: Acadia University, 1992.

Young, Tom. *"Fundy Shore Eco-Guide: A Traveller's Companion to the Fundy Shore."* Central Nova Tourist Association, 1995.

Index